OLGA WORRALL

Mystic With the Healing Hands

Olga Worrall

MYSTIC WITH THE HEALING HANDS

Edwina Cerutti

HARPER & ROW, PUBLISHERS

NEW YORK, EVANSTON
SAN FRANCISCO
LONDON

1817

FIRST EDITION

Designed by Sidney Feinberg

Library of Congress Cataloging in Publication Data

Cerutti, Edwina.
  Olga Worrall: mystic with the healing hands.
  1. Worrall, Olga Nathalie Ripich, 1906–
BF1027.W65C47 1975   133.9′092′4 [B]   75–9317
ISBN 0–06–061358–0

75 76 77 78 79 10 9 8 7 6 5 4 3 2 1

Contents

To my loved ones:
Here and There

The voice of God sounds in our ear:
Diffused, disturbingly unclear
And yet so sweet its roundelay
That few can hear and turn away.

E.C.

OLGA WORRALL

Mystic With the Healing Hands

CHAPTER I

Where Angels Fear to Tread

I WAS not a Spiritualist and I had never been one. I had never attended a seance, fooled with a Ouija board, or even talked to a medium. It is doubtful, in fact, if anything short of the terrible urgency surrounding my husband's illness would have ever swerved two such upright, solid, middle-class citzens as we were off the honored, well-paved path of orthodox medicine into the mysterious, tangled terrain of spiritual healing; and thence, into the even more mysterious world of the occult. But necessity makes for strange bedfellows indeed. Accordingly, poised like Hansel and Gretel before the door to the witch's cottage, we found ourselves one dark, windy October night hesitating outside a red-brick house in Baltimore, Maryland, wherein dwelt Olga and Ambrose Worrall—and our introduction to the psychic.

I had found the Worralls through their book *The Gift of Healing,* also called *The Miracle Healers,* which I had bought in a bookshop in a bus terminal in New York. John and I were en route to Maryland for the weekend and had stopped to browse in one of those huge paperback stores where the books, like groceries in a supermarket, are stacked according to subject. How I wandered into the realm of the supernatural I'll never know, but suddenly I realized I was in the midst of ghosts, ghouls, poltergeists, spirits and—supranormal healing.

My initial reaction was to laugh and call out to John who, as a physician, almost always managed to land in the science section: "Hey, sweetie, look what I found here!" My secondary reaction was more sober. Although John and I tried not to talk much about his condition, it was an endless prayer in my heart. There was nothing to lead either of us to believe that the pain in his back was a serious matter, but its strange persistence and increasing severity lay like a threatening black cloud over our heads; and I could never quite banish the uneasiness and fear that I felt.

Instead of laughing, therefore, I reached out and took *The Miracle Healers* from the shelf; attracted, perhaps, by the fact that the nondescript cover had none of the sexual or nightmarish decorative art which usually enhances so many paperbacks. With great doubt, nonetheless, I flipped the pages and read the opening words:

You can approach the undying flame, but you can never touch it. . . . the gifts of the Spirit are often unrecognized or misunderstood. One reason for writing this report on our healing ministry is our hope that others will be encouraged. . . . so that our lives, both physical and spiritual, become more meaningful for ourselves and others in the demonstration of Divine healing power.

Well! At least, this had none of the sound of a Danse Macabre, I thought, as I decided to buy the book and read it on the bus.

"What are you getting?" John asked, as I started for the cashier.

"Oh, just some book on spiritual healing by some people named Worrall," I replied. "Want to read it with me?"

"Spiritual healing?" he echoed incredulously. "You're not serious, are you?"

"And why not?" I countered. "There's no harm in seeing what it's about, anyway—and for less than a dollar."

"But, look here," John began, then suddenly stopped as he noticed the time on a wall clock. "Good God, let's hurry or we'll miss our bus. Go on and get it if you like—but move faster, please, or we'll never make it."

Within five minutes, therefore, we had made my purchase, rushed down to the lower level of the Port Authority Bus Terminal, boarded the bus, and settled back in a breathless but customary state of travelers' discomfort. Then, ignoring the rigid, almost cell-like confines in which I sat—fitted in like a coin in the slot of a vending machine—I opened the book I had just bought and began to read.

Mile after mile slid by, and page after page. Occasionally I would wake John up (sleep was his specific antidote for bus travel always!) and make him listen to some interesting excerpt; at other times I would rouse him long enough to elicit some critical comment. In a comparatively short while both of us were huddled over the little book, and there was no more talk.

"Good God!" It was John who spoke first as we neared the end of the Kennedy Highway and had gone more than halfway through the book. "I never heard such—such gobbledygook," he finally said, searching unsuccessfully for an appropriate word. "Did you?"

"Never," I agreed. "Ghosts in the bedroom and visions—"

"And instructions from beyond on spiritual healing!" John interrupted. "Those Worralls must be crazy! Or else, they must be out-and-out charlatans!"

"Or else," I finished for him, "they may be just telling the truth—however weird the truth may sound."

John was silent for a moment. "You don't really believe that, do you?" he asked thoughtfully. "You can't just swallow this kind of stuff, can you?"

It was my turn to think in silence then. "I don't know," I answered at last. "I truly don't know. All I do know, sweetie, is that anything is possible. Look, remember when television was ready for launching? Many people said it was ridiculous to think you could send pictures through the air. And radio met an equally solid, stubborn, resistant reaction. In fact, anything new and different usually runs into a solid wall of doubt, so why not this? Don't you see? I mean," I tried to explain in conclusion, "how can we sit here and condemn or deny the whole possibility without even knowing anything more about it?"

"I do see what you mean," John answered, "but you must admit the whole thing's pretty outlandish."

"It's incredible," I agreed. "But, honestly, so are all things that I can't visualize or touch. Take electricity, for instance. I've read about electrical waves in the air a thousand times, but because I can't see them, they're not real to me. Same thing about sound waves in radio: none of those things makes any sense—I mean, to me."

"But *ghosts?*" John asked pointedly. "Surely they're something else entirely."

"But why?" I dropped the closed book into my purse as I replied. "Scientific inventions are no less miraculous to me than clairvoyance. Maybe you feel you can understand scientific things because of your scientific background, but that doesn't prove a thing. It only proves that we all accept what we know something about and tend to turn from anything that falls within the realm of our own particular unknown."

That was the abrupt end to the discussion, however, since we had arrived by this time in the Baltimore terminal and we began, instead, to collect our few things in order to leave the bus. Nor, following this, was there any opportunity for further talk as we were swept forward into the flurry of being met and greeted. Then, of course, there were visitings and dinner and several hours of pleasant conversation—so that, in fact, I had quite forgotten the whole idea by the time we said a fond goodnight to our hosts and retired to the guest room assigned to us.

While undressing, though, and in the middle of some casual commentary on the evening, I stopped abruptly as I noticed the look of pain on John's face when he bent forward to undo his laces.

"Oh, darling," I said quickly, "is it your back?"

He nodded.

"Do you want some aspirin?" How pitifully small are the practical offerings of even the greatest love! "We have some in the suitcase. Should I get it?"

"I know. I'll take some soon," John answered. Then, looking at me earnestly, but with obvious embarrassment, he asked: "Do you really think it's worth bothering to see those people we were reading about on the way down? Those—what was their name?"

"Those Worralls." I remembered the name thoughtfully. "And why not?" I agreed. "Maybe they can help; and the good Lord knows they can't do any harm. It isn't as if you'd be abandoning some tried-and-true therapy for witchcraft. Nobody's been able to help you to date—and you've been to several specialists already. Besides, look at the coincidence of our being in Baltimore like this and my picking up that book. Right? What do you say to my trying to contact them tomorrow?"

"Well." The hesitancy in John's voice made me almost laugh.

"What's the matter?" I asked. "Afraid someone will find out?"

"Sort of," he admitted, smiling sheepishly. "Aren't you?"

"I tell you what," I promised. "We won't tell a soul. We'll just sneak off by ourselves and go. Let's get some sleep now and I'll phone the Worralls in the morning."

I did phone the Worralls the very next morning—since, fortunately, they were listed in the directory—but at first it seemed as if we had encountered a blank wall.

"I'm sorry," said the pleasant but unyielding voice on the other end of the line, "but you can't see Mr. Worrall at all. He no longer sees people directly. He's really retired."

"But this is very important," I insisted. "Won't you please ask Mr. Worrall and let him decide?"

"I'm Mrs. Worrall," replied the determined voice, "and I'll be happy to relay your message to Mr. Worrall so that he can pray for you in our regular nine o'clock quiet time. But he won't see you. He doesn't see anyone personally anymore."

For a moment this unexpected impasse seemed almost beyond resolution. Then I made one last try.

"Mrs. Worrall," I said, "my husband is a physician. We're here all the way from New York. I would not insist in this way if it weren't so urgent. Won't you please make an exception to your rule? Surely there must be some latitude for exception in your scheme of things, isn't there?"

A brief silence ensued, in which I could hear the metallic hum of the wires that stretched between us. Then Mrs. Worrall answered, almost abruptly, as if she had come to a sudden decision: "All right, dear. You and your husband come over tonight at seven o'clock. I'll leave the front porch light on. Do you have the address? Can you find your way?"

"I'll find it," I said. "And thank you for letting us come. We'll see you tonight at seven."

Jubilantly I replaced the receiver and went to tell John about our appointment—only to find that I had another selling job to do.

"I don't know about this," he kept saying, even when we were finally on our way, driving through the deserted streets in the dark. "People would say we're crazy, at the very least. Maybe we'd better not go."

"Rubbish," I scoffed. "Why should we care what people would say—especially when people don't know? I think we sneaked off very effectively, anyway. Don't you?"

"You bet," John laughed, forgetting to argue. "Like Secret Agent Smart fumbling with a new assignment! Oh well, we might as well go on. We're almost there."

We were by then in a quiet, residential part of the city, and the street at which we turned off the main thoroughfare was typical of the entire neighborhood. Neat, well-kept, trimmed hedges sat primly around comfortable, middle-class, brick-and-clapboard colonial dwellings. By the faint light of the scattered lampposts, stretches of smooth lawns could be seen; and from some nearby backyard barbecue, the odor of broiling beef and smoking charcoal filled the air.

"Well, sweetie," I said to John as he pulled up before a house displaying the proper number and a brightly lit, screened front porch, "you must admit this setting doesn't look like any voodoo business, does it? Do you still feel leery?"

"Of course," he said, opening the car door. "Let's go."

So we went: out of the car, across a concrete path, up the front steps—all of it as reassuringly commonplace and unextraordinary as a slice of apple pie or American cheese. Nevertheless, I know that my heart was beating more rapidly and uneasily as we stood hesitantly and close together—almost as if for comfort—in front of the closed door. What in God's name were we doing here? What kind of fantastic nonsense would we encounter? Was John right: were we a little out of our minds to be embarking on such an enterprise at all?

I think, in fact I almost know, that I was ready at this point to grab John's hand and dash back to the car and speed off into the night, straight back to the solid surburban world from which we had come. The door, however, was opened wide just then (our footsteps having been heard) and retreat was impossible. We stood, instead, like some passengers who had just landed from a hijacked plane, uncertain of where we were but most certain that having landed at last, there was nothing to do but get off.

CHAPTER II

Opening the Cauldron

I~T WAS~ Ambrose Worrall, primarily, whom John and I came to see; but it was Olga Worrall, eventually, whom I stayed to know. From the moment she opened the door for us, I was plagued by a relentless curiosity—perhaps, even, just because her appearance was so radically different from what we had both expected.

Certainly, the woman who stood on the threshold to welcome us was as far removed from discernible sorcery as Little Orphan Annie, or Charlie Brown. She was, instead, a rather matronly kind of person, neatly dressed in a casual but stylish fashion, with gray-streaked brown hair pulled back—but not tightly—into a bun, and with a figure that was just a little on the heavy-set side. Most distinctive was the warm, reassuring smile on her face that was soft and shining like candlelight in a dark place—so shining, in fact that it somehow seemed to light up her mahagony-colored eyes with an unusual brightness.

"Come on in, come on," she said in greeting. "I'm Olga Worrall and Ambrose will be down in a minute. Just choose yourselves a chair and we'll get acquainted."

I now know that it was always Olga's routine to act as a kind of buffer for Ambrose—sort of an unofficial master of ceremonies who undertakes to loosen up the audience before the star appears. I also now know—from experience—that it works.

"I'm Edwina," I answered awkwardly, as we followed her obediently into a comfortable living room.

"And I'm John," John said, seizing the cue. "I think my wife told you something about our situation over the phone when she called you this morning."

"Of course," she replied. "You see, we don't see people here anymore. After all, Ambrose is retired now. He's seventy. But there are always some exceptions, aren't there? Please do sit down."

I had been looking around, as Olga went on talking, heaving a huge, inward sigh of relief at the sight of the beautiful, flowered Persian rug on the floor and the brilliant reds and greens of a room that could have been a stage set for any Broadway play on surburbia.

"And, of course," Olga still went on speaking in her hearty manner, as we sat down, "ever since that book of ours was published, there's been no end of callers. Seems as if there's a terrible lot of suffering in this old world of ours, and people do need help, whatever kind of help they can get—even our kind! Right?"

She burst into infectious laughter that I soon came to realize punctuated many of her statements. As suddenly, though, she stopped, almost as if interrupted by someone or something.

"Is your father in the spirit world?" she asked John.

"The spirit world?" John repeated, obviously not understanding the question.

"Has your father passed on?" Olga explained patiently. "Because I see a man standing beside you and he says he is your father."

"Oh." For a moment, neither John nor I could say anything else. A man standing beside him? His father? Where? Obviously, there was no one there that either of us could see—and we both stared at Olga the way one tries not to stare at a

psychiatric patient when he is busy talking to himself or flick-
ing imaginary ants off his fingers.

Then I remembered that I had read that Olga was clairvoyant: could this be what clairvoyant meant? "Er—yes," I finally
managed to answer, since John seemed too uncomfortable
with this turn of events to speak for himself. "That is, John's
father is dead. He did pass on."

"Of course," Olga replied matter-of-factly. "Many years ago
—right? That's what he just told me."

"That *is* right," John was at last beginning to recover. "It
was a long time ago."

"So he says," Olga affirmed. "But he wants you to know that
he has always kept an eye on you and tried to help you whenever he could. He says it was his influence that made you
abandon your ideas of studying law and take up medicine. He
says you make an excellent doctor. He's very pleased with you,
in fact."

Now John and I looked with astonishment at each other.
How could she know that John had first so much considered
being a lawyer that he had once even enrolled at a law school
only to switch suddenly to medicine? How could she know
that? So long ago and so almost forgotten by both of us!

"Oh, another thing," Olga rambled on. "He was a very serious student himself, wasn't he? He says he was a teacher.
Correct?"

"Correct." There was utter amazement in John's voice. "Of
course, I never really knew him myself, but all of that is what
I've been told many times by those who knew him."

"Too bad you never knew him," Olga replied, as casually as
if she were talking about her nextdoor neighbor, "because he
certainly seems to be a very nice man. And he says to tell you
that he knows about your pain and that he is trying to get some
spirit doctors to help you." At this point she paused, and then
called out loudly: "Ambrose, come down, dear. Our visitors
are here."

From somewhere upstairs, a voice answered, "I'm coming," and we could hear the sound of footsteps, first on the floor above us, and then on the carpeted steps at the end of the room.

The sight of Ambrose next—he entered in just one more minute—was but another in this startling series of wholly preposterous events. As he was the heralded Master Magician in the piece, both John and I had every right to expect Merlin himself. The appearance, therefore, of a very unextraordinary intelligent-looking, heavy-set, sport-shirted man who seemed no more than sixty (although he had been billed as seventy!) and who had the happy smile of a Michelangelo cherub, was almost unnerving.

"Sit down, don't get up," he said in a soft voice with a decided English accent. "Let's just talk a bit before we go up to the healing room. Now, you just tell me about your problem and then I'll try to explain a bit about how we work—the kind of thing I do. . . ."

I could almost see John relax visibly at this approach. Giving a case history was strictly in accord with medical protocol, and he had no difficulty whatsoever in launching into a summation of the key points involved.

"So you see," he finally finished, "I've tried most everything medical science can suggest, but to no avail. I've had shots, medication, even some X-ray therapy. Name it and I've tried it up to today, and still nobody can help—or even really know just what I have. Which, in essence, is what brings me here to you."

Throughout John's recital, Ambrose had been listening intently and with the serious air of one clinician to another. Occasionally he had interrupted to ask some pertinent question that almost assumed a knowledge of John's condition that he could not have possibly known; most often, he just nodded his head affirmatively, more like a teacher verifying a pupil's performance in memorization than like someone being newly informed; and once he even made some slight correction.

At the end, he said, "Now let me explain what I'm all about," and proceeded to elaborate on what we had already read in his book: that he did not know exactly how his healing worked; that he followed entirely as the spirit led him (and he obviously meant this in a literal sense!); that he could only try to help but he could never guarantee results. Did we understand?

There was a dry, almost businesslike tone to Ambrose's address, and when he had completed his statement, it was Olga who said briskly: "Now, Ambrose, why don't you and John go upstairs to the healing room while Edwina and I wait here? How about that, honey," she asked, turning to me, "why don't we visit some more while the men get to work?"

So we "visited." Olga, that is, did most of the talking while I sat, obviously "on edge," twisting my handkerchief. For at least three quarters of an hour, her pleasant voice went on and on, with some head nodding from me and an occasional Yes or No. She told of the different healings Ambrose had accomplished: the doctor's wife who was dying of cancer until she came to Ambrose; the little girl whom he helped to make a complete recovery from meningitis; the young man who was raised from a bed of pain—and on and on.

With each new case she talked about, she seemed to be saying: "I know you're worried. Don't worry. See what's been done before. Maybe it can be done again." There was a warmth and an understanding in her voice that almost made me weep, the way unexpected kindness or relief often does when we stumble upon it in the midst of distress or despair.

With each new case she talked about, moreover, her obvious deep feeling for her husband seemed to be more predominant than anything else. It was as if she sat within a circle illuminated by her love for this man; it was as if this light of her love were the source spring of her life. Everything was Ambrose: Ambrose did this; Ambrose went there; Ambrose said that.

Suddenly, I could not help but interrupt. "And what about you?" I asked.

"Me?" So sincere was her dedication and devotion that she honestly did not know what I meant.

"You," I repeated. "You do healing, too, don't you? Didn't I read that you conduct the New Life Clinic, at a nearby Methodist church, for spiritual healing?"

"Of course!" the gay laughter burst forth again. "I hold clinic one day each week almost all year long. We've had tremendous experiences. Ambrose comes sometimes when he's free, and he and I—"

At this point, I laughed too. "There you go with Ambrose again. He is everything to you, isn't he?"

It was a strange thing, I now think, to be saying something like that to someone I had just met; but neither Olga nor I seemed to notice. Her friendliness was a genuine thing and her interest as sincere. Her reply, therefore, was equally uninhibited.

"He is everything," she answered thoughtfully. "Our twins passed on many years ago—you may have read that, too?"

"Oh yes, that was in the book," I remembered.

"So it's really the two of us—if you know what I mean." She smiled at me as she said this, somehow surely aware, in her usual unfathomable way, that I did know.

And I did. Even with our own houseful of seven children, I know only too well the scope and intensity of feeling that can grow between a man and a woman within the framework of a good marriage. Then it occurred to me: "It must have been terrible for you and Ambrose when both the twins died—within a few days of each other, I believe. Isn't that how it happened?"

"Within a few days," she affirmed, though without any great show of gloom. "But, of course, we've been in touch with them right along."

For a moment, this sudden return to things spiritualistic

made me almost gasp. I had practically forgotten, as we spoke, who and what Olga Worrall was. I seemed to see, instead, only a fellow human being—a human being whose open love for her husband and whose unabashed laughter in life would forever ensure her kinship with all women everywhere and in every time. Returning at her cue to the basic topic, however, but treading as cautiously as if walking down a narrow corridor marked "Wet Paint," I asked: "What do you mean that 'you've kept in touch with them right along'? How?"

"I mean," said Olga patiently, "that Ambrose and I have seen them many times in the spirit world. They're fine young men now, and we've been indeed privileged to watch them grow."

"To watch them grow?" I must have sounded like some empty echo emerging from a hollow cavern, devoid of human mind.

"Of course," replied Olga. "When they first passed on, Ambrose's sister—who had died a number of years before—came to us one night carrying the babies. She told us she would look after them for us, and she did."

"Oh." This was the most intelligent comment I could make.

"We've seen them many times," she went on happily. "Why, I had one of the most tremendous visits on my fiftieth birthday. It was on a November thirtieth, and we had gone to visit in Cleveland. In the bustle of arriving the day before, and seeing people, it had completely escaped me that the next day was my birthday. Then I was awakened at four o'clock in the morning by both my boys. They were standing at the foot of the bed in which Ambrose and I were sleeping. There was a group of people with them, and each of my sons held a bouquet of beautiful, brilliantly colored flowers in his hands—held it, incidentally, in exactly the way Ambrose holds a bouquet when he brings one. 'Happy birthday, Mom,' they said, and the other people said 'Happy birthday' also. It woke Ambrose up, too—and then they began to fade away gradually."

There was a long silence after Olga concluded her account. What could I say? Her eyes were sparkling with the memory, her voice was lifted with delight. Preposterous? Incredible? Insane? Perhaps; but as I looked at Olga, I knew that if this were delusion, it was self-delusion first.

"You really *saw* them?" I asked. "Or any of those people, like John's father, that you say you see? You're sure you don't just imagine them?"

Fortunately, Olga was not easily offended. "I know it sounds crazy to many people," she said, with a wry smile. "Don't I know it, though! But I do see things as clearly as I see you. Ambrose sees them, too, and frankly, it has shaped our whole lives. Most everyone has to grapple as long as they live with the idea of life and death; but for us, these things are facts. We know there is no death in the final sense that death is usually thought of, because we have had so much contact with those who have departed. We have, at times, made astral trips to the spirit world ourselves. Why, I can't begin to tell you about what we have seen and heard!"

"Ambrose, too?" I asked. "You mean he does these things, too? I thought he just did some kind of spirit healing."

"Honey," Olga laughed, "it's all part of the same whole! Ambrose was clairvoyant before he ever stumbled on his healing ability. And this healing ability of his—and mine—is obviously nothing that belongs to the three-dimensional world we inhabit on the physical plane. Good Lord, why does it astound people so? Didn't Jesus tell us about 'worlds within worlds'? Didn't Jesus operate above the so-called natural laws? What do you think happens when you pray?"

"I see what you mean," I replied slowly. "It certainly would seem logical that anyone who accepts the concept of God would automatically be acknowledging the concept of spirit."

Olga looked at me directly, challengingly. "Do you think

this little bit of life we live here is all? Do you think a physical body is the sum total of a man?" she asked.

"I guess not," I answered. "Any more than cutting off a patient's arms or legs destroys the person he is. There is an essence, an intelligence, a personality that continues to exist even when a body is half-dead. But even so," I went on earnestly, "is it really possible to bridge the gap between here and hereafter?"

Olga shrugged. "For some of us it is," she said simply. "For Ambrose and me it is—and heaven knows we each came by it separately, literally from two opposite ends of the earth."

"And yet you met and went on with it together!" I exclaimed. "That's a miracle in itself!"

"That it is," she said seriously. "Which is one of the reasons we felt that we had to dedicate ourselves and this power to helping people when we could. Fortunately, Ambrose has been a highly successful engineer—even on a consultant basis after his retirement—so that we never even felt the temptation to use our psychic gifts for gain. And just being able to do it together, to have each other's cooperation and understanding, has been our greatest blessing." She stopped abruptly then, as the clock on the piano began to chime nine o'clock. Immediately, raising her voice, she called out: "Ambrose, it's nine o'clock. You and John come on down here for our quiet time. Do you hear me, sweetie?"

From upstairs, Ambrose answered, "Coming!" and while they came, I remembered the book's description of their "quiet time." Every night, apparently, Olga and Ambrose ceased all activity at nine o'clock, during which period they prayed for those people who had placed themselves under their care.

As John and Ambrose entered the room, therefore, Olga got up and turned off the lights so that we were left sitting in a darkness that was as complete as the silence which promptly engulfed us. It was a strange silence, in a way almost alive with invisible vibrations; and I instinctively reached to John, who had seated himself beside me, for his hand. It was a peaceful silence, though, as well, almost as if we were in some distant haven, far removed from the metropolitan turmoil of a city like Baltimore.

"Ambrose," Olga said at last, "won't you close with a brief prayer?"

After the prayer, and when the lamps had been turned on again and we had finished blinking at the sudden light, Olga said to John: "I saw your father again in our quiet time. He was right beside your chair. Did you see him, Ambrose?"

"I did," declared Ambrose. "Looks like a fine sort of man."

I stole a quick glance at John while this was being said to gauge the reaction level on his shock meter. Amazingly, he appeared quite undisturbed, as if, in accordance with Hitlerian principles, to prove that anything repeated often enough, however false or unbelievable, becomes eventually acceptable. In any case, he only smiled at Olga and Ambrose, and then turned to me to say, "Darling, you'd never imagine how much basic medicine Ambrose knows. I've never met any lay person before with so much knowledge of anatomy and physiology."

"And why not?" laughed Olga. "We've been taught by the best scientists in the spirit world. Did Ambrose tell you what they told me about cancer years ago?"

"No." John looked at her expectantly.

"Well," Olga began, "years back, in several conversations with some spirit doctors, I was told most definitely that one form of cancer in particular is a viral disease. They said that researchers here were looking in all directions for a knowledge of how to cure cancer, but that they had not yet hit on the correct answer because they had missed the fundamental point. They also told me that the mycin drugs often triggered cancers, too, by disturbing the blood chemistry of the body."

"That is interesting," John replied. "Certainly, the viral etiology of cancer is one of the dominant research theories today. A tremendous amount of investigative work is being done in that area right now."

Just then the telephone rang and Olga excused herself to go into the adjoining room to answer it. As we waited for her return, we could clearly hear her side of the conversation. "Hello," she said. "No, I'm sorry, but Mr. Worrall can't come to the phone. . . . I'm sorry, but he can't see you. He's retired. Why don't you tell me your problem and I'll relay it to him and we'll hold you in our thought in our quiet time. . . . Yes . . . I see. Well look here, honey. We'll work for you, but you'd better get yourself in hand first and stop drinking. Things will look a lot different to you when you do . . . of course. . . . Right. . . . Now what's your name? . . . Yes . . . good. God bless you. Goodbye."

As Olga returned to the living room, she said: "That call was from California. I made a note of it on the pad, Ambrose, and we'll take it up later." Then turning to us again, she said, "Where was I? Oh yes, about cancer being a virus—can you imagine, I was told about that almost twenty years ago—way before medical men even were really thinking along those very lines! And they've only gotten to it rather recently."

"Did you mention it to anyone?" I asked Olga.

"Honey," she laughed gaily, "they'd sooner listen to someone from the looney bin! Oh, I mentioned it all right, but—" and she shrugged eloquently.

At this point, the telephone rang again and Olga went off to answer it once more. This time it was obviously someone who had called before, because Olga asked specific questions about the individual case, reiterated some previous advice about "leaving that man before he beats you up again," promised continued effort on the caller's behalf, and hung up.

"Oh, dear," she said as she resumed her seat, "I do hope it isn't going to turn into one of those telephone evenings."

"What do you mean?" I asked.

"Just that some evenings, the phone gets started and never stops. People call and call—from everywhere and anywhere. We even get some from Australia, that far away."

"And you handle them all?" I asked. "For you and Ambrose?"

"Of course," she replied.

"And the letters, too," Ambrose added.

"What letters?" I hadn't even thought of the mail approach.

"Goodness," Olga explained, "most people write us rather than call. We get mail—hundreds of pieces a week—from all over the world, and I answer them all."

"All?" I repeated increduously.

"All," she answered firmly. "When people call out for whatever help, whatever encouragement we can give, we feel it's just our duty to respond. Don't you see?"

"Of course, I see," I said. "But it's such a heroic job! I know, because one of the books, in particular, that I wrote several years ago elicited great public reaction, and I found it absolutely impossible to handle the mail that came in, even though I wanted to."

"It is heroic," Olga agreed cheerfully, "but I do it."

"She certainly does," Ambrose said. "And does it, in spite of our being out of town so much, lecturing, and holding healing sessions at the New Life Clinic.

"You are amazing," I told Olga sincerely. Then, as the clock struck ten, and I realized how long we had stayed, I stood up, and John did, too, in order to go. "We've taken too much of your time already," I apologized to Olga and Ambrose, "but I'm just so full of questions—"

"Like what?" asked Olga, standing up also.

"Like—well, how does your clairvoyance work? What is

your own reaction to it? What do you know of the spirit world? What's it like—according to what you think you've seen? How do people react to what you say? What is your reaction to their reaction?" I stopped abruptly, and finished with: "Oh, I could go on and on!"

"You are full of questions," Olga laughed.

"I hope you don't mind," John interspersed for me. "But, as you can see, Edwina's never met up with a—with someone like you before—"

"And I am intrigued!" I interrupted.

"But still full of reservations?" Olga asked, jokingly. "And I didn't need any second sight to see that!" she added, with a big smile.

"Still full of reservations?" I repeated her question aloud. "I honestly don't know. Still full of questions, though, and that's for sure! You see, you've lived with all of this for so long—"

"For all of my life," Olga said.

"—that you probably forget," I went on, "how absolutely incredible all of this can be to someone on the outside."

"Oh, I never forget at all," Olga said, as she and Ambrose followed us to the door. "Every lecture hall is filled with the skeptics and the curious, and only a handful of believers to help leaven the bread."

By this time, we were all standing in the doorway. Ambrose shook hands with John and said, "Let me hear how you do," and John replied, "I definitely will. And are you still insistent on refusing any remuneration?"

"I certainly am," Ambrose declared emphatically. "No, no! We never take any money. God has given us all we need, and we are happy to use such gifts as we have been blessed with to help others. Isn't that so, Olga?"

"Of course," she replied immediately. Then, turning to me, she said sincerely, "I am very glad you came."

"So am I," I said, trying to explain how I felt. "It's as if I've opened a door that looks into another world, a strange world —so strange, in fact, that I can't help wondering if it actually exists at all!"

"It is another world," said Olga, "but it's also part of this."

"And I do hope," I went on, somewhat self-consciously, "that you really don't mind all those questions of mine."

For answer, Olga put her arms about me and kissed me goodbye. "Of course, I don't mind," she said warmly. Then, as we at last started down the front path, she called out laughingly: "Come back whenever you can and ask all the questions you like. Ask enough questions even to fill a book!"

And though I did not know it then, as I waved a farewell, this parting statement was Olga's final clairvoyant prediction for the night.

CHAPTER III

A Visit to the Battlefront

I CAME BACK to see Olga Worrall many, many times and over a period of years. I watched and listened and probed with all the intensity of a Dr. Livingstone attempting to penetrate darkest Africa. What's more, I came away with the unshakable conviction that it can be easier to explore a vast continent than to get to really know a single human being.

Piece by piece, however, I did get to really know Olga Worrall. My starting point was the New Life Clinic which Olga conducts every Thursday morning at ten in the Mount Washington Methodist Church of Baltimore. My first visit, in fact (and I have been to many), was enough to provide a complete baptismal immersion into the concept of spiritual healing which is Olga's forte.

The church itself is not overly impressive. It is obviously old and somewhat musty, although its very age does seem to have saturated the sanctuary where we gathered with almost tangible emanations from the vast amounts of living and dying that must have happened there. The wooden pews hold about three hundred fifty in all; and the ancient organ up ahead plainly has a few mute keys which stand out as glaringly in its playing as some missing front teeth do in any face.

My initial visit took place on a gloomy, icy day. When I entered, however, the place was already quite full and I walked slowly down the aisle to get myself a front-row seat, as befits a critic and researcher on opening night. As I walked, moreover, I took advantage of the opportunity to observe and appraise the crowd quickly.

There were definitely a greater number of women than men—but not disproportionately so. There were, also, a greater number of middle-aged and older people present, but there were quite a few younger ones, too. Several children, scattered throughout, sat next to watchful parents; and in a front pew, just inches away from me, was a Catholic priest, about thirty years old, and an Anglican minister visiting (as I later discovered) from England.

Even after I sat down, I turned boldly around to look. After all, I was no convert but a practical investigator and if there were mostly kooks here, it was my duty to so note and report. How valid could testimony of spiritual healings be if the witnesses to the healings were unreliable or unsound?

Apparently, though, there weren't. An occasional beard could be seen, of course, and a few heads of overlong, unkempt hair. The overwhelming majority of the congregation, however, were so clearly within the realm of the ordinary and the average that they might have emerged from the local A & P. In appearance, for instance, there was very little of the "Sunday-go-to-meeting" finery, but a thorough mixture of everyday suburban and work-clothes dress. Similarly, there was an obvious, wide representation of all kinds and types of people from housewives and doctors to clergymen and plumbers.

What was distinctive about the group as a whole was the serious attitude with which they sat and the expectancy with which they waited. The church was quiet but I could almost feel the silent prayers which filled it and which made me suddenly uncomfortable in my role of spy. I did not know and could not imagine what need had brought each petitioner here. It was enough for me to sense the composite need, just as it was impossible not to respect it.

In the midst of this thinking, Olga Worrall came sailing

down the aisle in a long, black academic robe that flowed
behind her. She took her stand in front of the middle of the
first pew with a broad, happy smile on her face that lit the
place up like a burst of sunlight in a darkened room.

"For heaven's sake," she began, "but you're all as crazy as
I am! Going out in this terrible weather! Why, isn't the Good
Lord right on the job, getting us all here safely? What do you
say to that for our beginning today?"

She burst out laughing and we all laughed with her. Then
she went on:

"Okay now, let's get down to business. First, let me say that
there are no guaranteed healings. We have had cases that are
like miracles; we've had others that have been greatly helped;
and we've had others that were untouched. Why? I don't
know—and that's mostly because it is not I who heals, but the
spiritual power that comes from God. I put my hands on you
and pray, but it is God who does the work."

Then, apparently because so many new people come to the
sessions each week, she briefly explained the procedure they
followed. From 10:00 to 10:30, Olga speaks and answers any
questions that are asked; from 10:30 to 11:00, there is time for
meditation and prayer while the organ softly plays; from 11:00
to 12:00, a brief sermon is delivered by the minister of the
church, or by a visiting minister, following which Olga, as-
sisted by the minister and another worker, Fred Orenschall (if
these men are present), administers the laying-on of hands for
healing to those who come forward. After the service, a light
lunch is served on the church lower floor for all who stay and
pay the modest luncheon fee.

"Now," said Olga, after these preliminaries, "let's get back
to you and me. Most of you are here because you need healing
and you need it so desperately that you'll even take spiritual
healing. Well, that's fine. But do you really have any faith? Yes
and no. You do and you don't. You're like the woman in the
Bible who said to Jesus: 'Lord, I believe; help thou mine un-

belief.' When you come up and ask to be healed, do you really think God will do it or are you really saying, Maybe?"

For the next twenty minutes or so, Olga developed this point. She poked away at the secret doubt that unfortunately so often is the mote in the eye of almost every believer, and that somehow invariably manages to corrode the most staunch, iron-clad faith—but she did it with love and understanding and humor.

Her conclusion was direct and simple. "Faith is power," she said, "so you've got to work away at it and develop it as you would any muscle. And, while you're doing that, keep remembering how wonderful and caring God is: that even with our weak, flimsy faith, he answers so many prayers! He grants so many healings! Okay?" She paused expectantly and asked: "Who has any questions?"

Over on the side, in one of the back rows, a man raised his hand and said: "You say 'develop faith.' But can you tell us how? Isn't it easier said than done?"

"You bet it is!" Olga laughed as she replied. "That's the jackpot question and there's no easy answer, no magic formula that will give you Instant Faith the way you can make instant coffee. You have to work at it unceasingly, through daily prayer and meditation and affirmation. Gradually, slowly, your persistence will be rewarded and the feeling of conviction within you will grow and grow and grow. But nothing will happen if just every once in a while—like, say, on a Sunday morning—you direct your thoughts to God. No sir! If you want a strong body, you exercise. Well, prayer is exercise for the spirit the same way walking is exercise for the body." She then looked around: "Who's next?"

Many were next, and Olga answered each in turn: promptly, surely, and "with authority." The questions were no idle ones, either, but serious, thoughtful attempts to learn and understand.

Finally Olga called an abrupt halt. "Children," she said,

"we're out of time. Let's settle down for silent meditation and prayer and make ourselves ready for the healing service."

Almost immediately, the organ music began and a complete silence fell over the worn old church. Some people, obviously Catholic, went up and knelt at the altar rail, making the sign of the cross as they did so; others sat in their places with closed eyes; and still others, like me (probably newcomers!), looked quietly around at everyone else.

At eleven sharp, Olga and the Reverend Bob Kirkley and the Reverend Bob Cartwright (visiting) and Fred Orenschall, began the healing service. After a short sermon by Kirkley and one hymn, the three men and Olga stood spaced out behind the altar rail and Olga invited those who wished to come up for healing to do so.

One by one, then, they came. Each in turn went and knelt before either Olga or one of the men, and as they moved forward individually, I could see them better. One woman pushed her little boy forward to kneel before Olga, after which she watched anxiously from a nearby pew. One man, about fifty, white and emaciated and as clearly marked by illness as a leper by his sores, was led to Olga by what was obviously a much concerned member of his family, probably a younger brother. A thin, pale-faced fortyish woman limped by to take her place in the waiting line.

It was an impressive, silent procession, about three hundred people long. Nothing was said aloud. For each person Olga had a smile so filled with encouragement and compassion that even I could sense its radiating warmth. Occasionally she would exchange a few whispered words with a newcomer. In all cases, she would close her eyes and put her hands on the person before her, standing in this position for at least two or three minutes. The places where she laid her hands varied, although I couldn't tell why, but her parting, murmured "God bless you" was the same for all.

So intently was I watching, that my neck began to hurt. Several years before, I had sustained a bad whiplash injury in an automobile accident and the recurrent pain in my neck, which extended along to my shoulders, was something I had learned to live with the way one does with the annoying but inescapable nagging of a husband or a wife. There was nothing to do but bear it—which I always did with the help of some aspirin, since each new attack lasted for many hours.

"Ugh," I thought to myself, as the discomfort began that morning in the church, "Here we go again."

As unobtrusively as I could, therefore, I squirmed about some in my seat in an effort to shift the pull of my neck muscles and so alleviate the pain until I could get to some medication —but I did it almost automatically and without any real feeling of disturbance. I had been down this road too many times before to be deflected now from my self-imposed mission and I held steadfast to my observation post.

At this moment, however, the woman beside me in the pew stood up to go forward for healing. As she rose, she seemed to wait for me to get up also. She looked at me expectantly, her very hesitation seeming to say, "After you." Suddenly I thought in silent response, "Why not?"

Heaven knows I had never intended to join the line or take any part in the service. I was an investigator, not a participant. My role was fixed. Still: what better way to investigate than to participate? Besides, while I could see clearly enough from where I sat, there was not very much really to be seen. People went up and got down on their knees on the cushioned step below the altar rail; Olga placed her hands on them. There were no rays visible, no thunderclaps, no overt, dramatic reactions. Why not go up and see what, if anything, there was to see or feel?

Even as I moved forward, though, I was not as immune to the power that filled the sanctuary as I tried to pretend to myself. Jesus said that wherever three or more gathered in his name, there he would be. Well, something was in this gathering beyond any doubt, an intangible, invisible something that seemed to generate an emotional force of its own. I saw it on the faces of the hushed congregation; I felt it in the air around me; and I was most conscious of it as Olga placed her hands upon me.

When I resumed my seat, however, it was with almost a sense of disappointment. Escept for an unusual degree of heat that seemed to generate from Olga's hands, nothing had happened, at least as far as I could see. I found myself wondering if anything special had happened to anyone who had come there that day or was there just a mild kind of mass, religious hysteria permeating us all.

As I turned my head to look about, I suddenly became aware that the pain in my neck was *gone.* The realization astounded me. Impossible! Whenever that pain recurred, it persisted for hours, but now it had vanished. Incredulously, I craned my neck in all directions and gyrated my head in several ways to test for any twinges until it must have looked ridiculously like a telescope searching frantically for enemy craft from a submerged submarine. The fact remained: the pain was definitely gone.

Although I couldn't understand it at all and did not know then that it would never return, just the idea that something unusual had taken place was enough to unnerve me. It was enough, also, to make me realize how closed a mind I had brought to this service and how subconsciously certain I must have been that spiritual healing was utter bosh. Not that I was convinced yet; only that I had honestly begun to wonder.

By this time, the organ music sounded forth again, and most of the crowd headed for the lower floor of the church.

"Are you staying for lunch?" the woman next to me asked.

Before I could answer, Olga rushed over and said: "Edwina,

honey! I'm so glad you came! And are you still asking questions?"

"More than ever," I replied laughingly.

"Wonderful." Her response was wholehearted. "Then you must stay for lunch. Did you know that we have a whole group of older women in this church—in their seventies, as a rule, and up—who volunteer their services to cook and serve a hot lunch? It's really a grand idea because people can eat together and talk together after the service, in this way, and get a better feel for what's going on. Look here," she finished, leading me towards the stairs, "why don't you go down and sit at the head table with me? You'll meet some people worth talking to. And now I'm off to say Hello to some folks who can't stay. But you go on. I'll see you later."

It was actually only twenty minutes or so afterward when Olga came and sat beside me at the designated table, but it was a twenty minutes filled with fascinating observations. The lower floor of the church, where lunch was to be served, was the typical downstairs of any church, vintage 1860: neat, a little shabby, and as starkly simple as a Grandma Moses painting. Across and around the room were plain, straight wooden tables covered with paper tablecloths and set with paper plates; and gathered at these tables were at least half of the people who had been present at the healing service just before.

Most impressive, though, was the liveliness that rose almost like a happy song from one end of the room to the other. The spriest group of older women ran gaily about, depositing huge bowls (family style) of potato salad and cole slaw and meatballs on the tables, and then pausing to discuss matters with the diners. People who were obvious strangers to each other (I could hear the self-introductions) laughed and talked like long-standing friends.

"Is this your first time here?" one man asked his neighbor.

"It is," was the reply. "My wife's cousin says she got cured of bad sinus trouble by that Worrall woman, so I thought I'd try coming too."

From the other side of the room, I caught this rejoinder: "Now me," it was a woman speaking, "I find I pray best when I start with meditation. I do it like this. . . ."

How she did it was drowned out by a burst of laughter nearby, and I turned instead to look at the three men and two women who were seated with me. One was the young Catholic priest I had noticed upstairs; another turned out to be a visiting Anglican minister; and the third was the Reverend Bob Kirkley, paster of the Mount Washington Methodist Church. Of the two women who were there also, the younger was so openly and earnestly engaged in a conversation with our "waitress" that I did not have to listen in order to hear. Nor did anyone else.

"Now, dearie," the elderly food-bearer was saying, "let me just tell you what happened to me. About eight years ago it was. I found a lump in my breast one day and went right to the doctor. He didn't like it one bit and said he'd have to operate. While I was waiting to go into the hospital—must have been a week—my sister-in-law took me to the New Life Clinic. She belonged to the church here, you see, and knew about the healing services. Anyway, I came. Olga Worrall put her hands on me, right over the lump, and by the time I got back to my seat, the lump was gone. When I went back to the doctor, he couldn't believe it at first. Then he examined me and canceled the operation."

The woman who was the target of this object lesson listened attentively along with the rest of us. She was in her midthirties, one of those "China doll" blue-eyed blondes, and quite obviously dressed in beautiful, expensive clothes. Her diamonds flashed as she moved her hands worriedly.

"I don't know what to do," she sighed. "I'm supposed to go into the hospital next Wednesday for a biopsy—at the least. My doctor would think I'd lost my mind if I even postponed the surgery while I tried spiritual healing."

We all looked at her sympathetically.

"I've come all the way from Richmond to see Mrs. Worrall. You see, she cured my son in one visit three years ago. I had taken him to some of the biggest men at Hopkins and no one could help him. He had become a psychiatric case after one LSD session in college: depressed, deluded, and acting like one possessed. Well, Mrs. Worrall gave him one spiritual treatment and said something to him. When we returned to the pew, he was his old self again and he's been wonderful ever since. It was like a miracle, like Jesus casting out the demons. . . . But what do I do now?"

As she finished speaking, Olga came up and plopped herself down. She apparently had caught the question because she promptly replied: "Honey, no one can advise you. It has to be your own decision and no one can make it for you."

The woman who was serving and who had furnished her own case history before Olga's arrival, said enthusiastically: "I told her what happened to me!"

Olga laughed appreciatively. "Now, Millie," she said firmly, "Don't you go trying to influence Mrs. Roberts. Do you hear?"

Millie nodded vigorously and hurried away to the next table. Then Olga addressed us all: "Boy, am I hungry! What's for lunch today?"

While she inspected and helped herself, I resumed my role of the Inquiring Reporter. "Does the healing service exhaust you?" I asked, as an opener.

"Lord, no!" she replied. "It exhilarates me. I feel seven feet tall. I'm just a channel for the healing power, but the power comes from spiritual sources, not from me. Why should it tire me? Look here, Timmy," she said suddenly to the young priest, "why don't you try to answer this girl's questions so I can eat in peace?"

I looked from her to Father Timothy, a big-sized, reddish-

haired young man. "I don't really know that much yet," he
protested.

"Have you been coming to the New Life Clinic for a long
time?" I asked him next.

"Oh no," he answered, "only a few times. But I've been
attending the workshop sessions Olga holds through the
Spiritual Frontiers Fellowship. I'm here to learn."

"Learn what?" I was almost inexcusably persistent.

"Learn all about spiritual healing," he stated matter-of-
factly.

"And what made you decide to do that?"

"Well," he tried to explain, "there's a woman in my church
who came in for Mass one day. She told me about the New Life
Clinic and how she had been healed of deafness. And she
wanted to know why our church couldn't have helped her;
why she couldn't have had a priest do the laying-on of hands
just as the ministers do here, after Olga has led the way. Her
story intrigued me so much that I decided to see what it was
all about. Do you know what I mean?"

He paused; and I nodded. I knew only too well what he
meant.

"Well," he continued, "I began with Olga's lectures. They
were like a revelation. She made me aware for the first time
that spiritual healing is not only part of Jesus' ministry and the
New Testament practices, but of the Old Testament and the
prophets, too. I realized that even in the administering of the
last rites of the church, I had an opportunity to offer spiritual
healing. I determined to find out how."

His eyes shone with excitement as he spoke.

"And have you found out how?" I asked.

"I'm learning," he said earnestly. "Used to be, when I visited
the sick, it was all just rote. You know: words and gestures like
a marionette. But now I really pray. Now I'm conscious that
there is a spiritual power that can be channeled to help these

people—like the power that was all around us during the service upstairs. Didn't you feel it?"

"Well—sort of," I answered cautiously.

"Huh!" Olga interrupted, explaining to Father Timothy, "She's still a skeptic. She wants to see the dead raised before her very eyes—and even then she'd try to rationalize it away."

She was only half-serious, of course, but I felt called upon to defend myself anyway. "That's not really fair," I protested jokingly. "I'm just trying to find out some facts. For example: were any people healed upstairs today? Did anything more than a religious exercise take place?"

Olga groaned in reply. "Honey," she said, "how would I know? Some results show up gradually over several weeks. Even in some immediate healings, people often don't tell us; at least not right away. Sometimes they think they're only imagining improvements; other times they want to get medical confirmation before making any claims. And some people are just embarrassed to issue public proclamations about anything as foolish as spiritual healing."

This last statement made me feel definitely uncomfortable as I remembered my pain-free neck. Not only that I had *not* mentioned it, but that, if I could help it, I didn't intend to!

"Then, how do you judge effectiveness?" I asked.

"Oh, Edwina," Olga stated emphatically, "we do find out. Take letters, for instance. We get stacks of mail and mixed in with the requests for healings are hundreds of thank-you notes expressing gratitude for healings we've never even known about.

"Same thing goes for telephone calls. Someone will call and say, 'Last year, you helped me when I wrote to you about my arthritis. Would you please pray now for my daughter?' Well, she had written about her arthritis, but she had never bothered to write again to let us know that she had regained the use of her hands, and that she could walk again without any difficulty—I'm quoting from an actual case."

At this point, the Anglican minister from England spoke up. He was sitting across the table from Olga and me, but his remarks were apparently addressed to Olga. "I'm Father Wellesly," he said, "just arrived two weeks ago from just outside of London, and—"

"So you're Father Wellesly!" Olga interrupted. "I was wondering if you made it. I'm delighted that you're here!" Then Olga explained to the rest of us. "Father Wellesly called me yesterday to talk some and to ask me how to get here. Well, you know how I am about directions! I'm like a horse with blinders on. Start me at my house and I can follow a rote path and arrive, but put me one block off course and I get swallowed up by the streets—never to be heard from again!"

We all laughed—especially I. As usual, just that very morning, I had become hopelessly lost four times on my way to the church in spite of a written set of directions and a hand-drawn map with enough detail to chart a space ship to the moon.

Then Olga continued: "Father Wellesly is here from England to interview spiritual healers and to do research into the whole field."

"Precisely." The clipped, British tones matched the neat, angular face. He was fiftyish, slim, and obviously filled with his mission.

"Is this a church project you're on?" I interposed, wanting to maintain proper perspective and to sort things out in correct order.

"Not at all," he responded. "This is entirely my own. I was very much like this young man here," and he motioned to Father Timothy. "Until about one year ago, I had never really paid any attention to this kind of thing. Heard something occasionally, of course, but thought it must be rubbish or hysteria. Then one day, one of my parishioners, who was crippled up with some vascular disease and gout—real bent over, he was—came to me and asked what I thought of his trying a spiritual healer since medicine had been unable to help him. Poor fellow was a mess; so I said, not even paying it any mind, 'Why not?' and forgot all about it. Well, he did. And three weeks later, he comes in to see me and he's walking straight and tall and with a spring in his step.

"Shook me up, it did!" Father Wellesly smiled at the memory. "Got me started on finding out what this whole business is all about."

"And what have you been finding out?" I asked, as he paused.

"Everything!" he exclaimed. "I'm just back from eight days in California and I've seen enough to know that incredible healings have taken place and are happening every day. Healings that defy medical rationale. Spiritual healing is for real. It's not just a matter of the imagination."

"Imagination!" Millie was back now, pouring coffee. "You don't have to tell me that!"

"Or me either," affirmed the woman from Richmond.

"Oh, I'm convinced!" Father Wellesly assured them. "And what's being accomplished here is the same that's being accomplished in England. What I want to do now is collect some kind of evidence, practical and scientific, so that we can start meetings like the one upstairs today for our members. Reverend Mr. Kirkley," he said, turning to the pastor who had taken part in the service that morning, "how did this church of yours get into the healing ministry in the first place? And what does your Methodist bishop think of it all anyway?"

Bob Kirkely, who had been eating and listening throughout the entire table conversation (he'd said, and it was obvious, that he had missed breakfast), swallowed another mouthful and grinned. "It was really Olga's doing. She organized one with Dr. Day in the Mount Vernon Place Methodist Church right here in Baltimore. It impressed me so much that I asked her to join me in setting one up in my church when Dr. Day retired. And she did. As for the bishop: not only is he for it, but I believe he or his wife, or maybe even both of them, have had Worrall healings themselves. Am I right, Olga?"

Olga laughed merrily. "God heals, Bob," she reminded him. "I'm only a treatment channel. And I won't answer your question, either. Such matters are confidential."

Father Wellesly pursued his own objective. "Mrs. Worrall," he announced, "as I told you on the telephone, I'm here to learn. I don't know how it all works; I don't know why; and I don't know what it is that works. I only know that healing is part of God's work, that Jesus told us to go and do likewise. I feel most strongly that I must start a healing service in my own church back home; that it is my duty to my parishioners. Will you teach me how?"

By now, lunch was over and the hall was growing quite noisy as chairs were pushed back and people began milling about and saying goodbye. In answer to Father Wellesly's question, therefore, Olga pushed back her own chair and stood up.

"Look here," she said, "we can't really talk in this place. Of course, I'll be glad to help in any way that I can, so why don't you follow me in your car back to my house and we can have a regular jam session."

Father Wellesly nodded happily and promptly arose. Olga turned to the woman from Richmond, then, and said: "Honey, no one can tell you what to do. Why don't you pray about it and decide either to wait or go to surgery as the Lord leads you? He will. And let me know your decision. One way or the other, I'll hold you in my prayers. God bless."

She turned next to say goodbye to Bob Kirkley and to the other woman at our table who had not spoken once but whom Olga apparently knew. At Father Timothy's side, she stopped suddenly and said: "Timmy, why don't you come along home with me, too? After all, you and Father Wellesly are headed for the same goal. Right? Maybe your questions will help him see something and his questions will help you see something else. Want to come?"

"Wonderful!" the young man jumped up as he answered.

Then Olga looked me straight in the eye, as if I had spoken aloud. "Okay, honey," she said through a burst of laughter. "You come, too."

I had not said a word and I did not now in reply. As I gathered my coat and purse together, though, in preparation for our departure, it suddenly occurred to me—but this time without surprise—that once again Olga Worrall had read my mind. As suddenly, I realized how much more difficult for me was this task upon which I was already embarked: to read hers.

CHAPTER IV

Anatomy of a Mystic

THE CONCEPT of spiritual healing is not subject to scientific analysis or proof. It is an intangible defined in terms of intangibles and recognizable only by its concrete results, which are unfortunately always open to the charge of coincidence or self-delusion or honest error. Unsurprisingly, therefore, it was with this preface that Olga Worrall opened her impromptu lecture that afternoon.

"Look here," she began, as the two clergymen and I settled ourselves comfortably in her library after arriving at her home, "we can talk about spiritual healing from here to forever, but we can't even define it—much less prove it. It is *spiritual* healing primarily because of its dissociation from *material* methods of healing, which include all doctoring and drugs. It is the power of God channeled into healing, but it's no more visible or provable than God himself. And that," she added wryly, almost as an aside, "is an unfortunate fact that leaves the field wide open for all kinds of frauds and quacks."

Father Wellesly promptly agreed. "Indeed it does!" he exclaimed. "Why, even in my research there was one lady I observed at work" (and he mentioned a name obviously familiar to Olga) "who heals by doing a kind of belly dance with her hands up and down and all around her patient—never touching, mind you, but just waving her arms almost rhythmically like a ballerina in *Swan Lake*. And there was a man—presumably trained for healing in Tibet—who built up what he called his 'healing energy' by jumping and shrieking so violently that I was absolutely certain he would kill either himself or the man who had come for healing. I must say," Father Wellesly concluded, "it was most weird!"

We all laughed at his descriptions, which Father Timothy corroborated. "Just the other night," he said, "I saw some kooks like that demonstrating their 'art' on television. It certainly didn't look for real to me. What do you think?" he asked Olga.

"Well," she replied slowly, "I'm afraid my approach is nowhere that colorful. I do agree, though, that all that hokey-pokey tends to make spiritual healing look phony. But even some of these 'way-out' healers do have something. The trouble is that they've made it into a business and they try to give their 'customers' a run for their money. Personally, I've been blessed with a wonderful husband who has always provided so amply for me that I have never had to accept one cent for any of my healing services and I have never felt any need for embellishment to impress anyone."

At this point, Olga paused for a moment, then returned briskly to her general discussion. "Getting back to spiritual healing," she said, "you saw the healing service this morning. Now let me try to explain to you what it is that happens and why."

According to Olga, spiritual healing is the channeling of energy into a recipient from the universal field of energy which is common to all creation and which stems from the universal source of all intelligence and power, called God. Emanations surround each individual, apparently caused by electrical currents flowing in the physical body. There are sound waves from the various physical organs and thought waves from the mind as well as vibrations from the spiritual body. Energy from the universal field of energy becomes available to the healer through the act of tuning his personal energy field to a harmonial relationship with the universal field of energy so that he acts in this way as a conductor between the universal field of energy and the patient.

"Now remember," Olga finished laughingly, "I'm no scientist and I don't really understand what everything I've just said is all about. But this is what the spirit world has told Ambrose and me. Of course, Ambrose, as a scientist, has always made sense of this explanation. He says that spiritual healing is a rearrangement of the microparticles of which all things are composed. The body is not what it seems to be with the naked eye. It is not a solid mass. It is actually a system of little particles or points of energy separated from each other by space and held in place through an electrically balanced field. When these particles are not in their proper place, then disease is manifested in that body. Spiritual healing is one way of bringing the particles back into a harmonious relationship—which means, into good health."

As Olga paused for breath, I quickly asked the question that had hit me hardest while she had been speaking. "You've just finished saying that all of this explanation is what the spirit world has told you and Ambrose," I reminded her. "What does that mean?"

"Exactly what I said," was the immediate reply, "and I'm glad you brought it up. My kind of spiritual healing, you see, has a psychic overlay. When I lay my hands on someone seeking healing, I often receive, psychically, background information or even a diagnosis that helps me know what to say, therapeutically, to a patient, or what to do."

"But how do you 'receive' this information?" I persisted. "Do you hear voices?"

"Not in the usual sense you're referring to," Olga said laughingly. "Mostly it's that specific thoughts are impressed on my consciousness so clearly and so definitely that I have the un-equivocal feeling that someone has said something to me. Sometimes I actually hear a voice communicating. It's none that you would hear, though, because I sense it with my inner ear only. And still other times I actually see a spirit form near the person with the problem, and get messages from this spirit man or woman which are relevant to the problem and benefi-cial in its treatment."

The ringing of the telephone sent Olga scurrying to the far end of the library to answer it and there was nothing for the three of us to do in the interval but listen, somewhat self-consciously, to her side of the conversation.

"Wonderful! Wonderful!" she kept saying. "I'm so happy to hear it. Isn't it marvelous? Thank you for letting me know honey, and God bless!"

"Now there's a perfect example of what I was telling you all!" Olga's face beamed as she returned to us. "This woman called me a few days ago from Long Island in New York. Her father—in his seventies—was in great pain with a large stone in the kidney. The doctor was reluctant to operate because of the man's age and general condition, but there didn't seem to be any other way. The woman was so worried about the pro-posed surgery that she asked me to pray.

"Well, while I was talking to her on the phone, I suddenly saw—with my inner eye—a picture of the stone breaking down and being passed through the ureters. At the same time I was informed that, if surgery were withheld for a couple of days more, it would be totally unnecessary as the man would be healed in this way with spiritual help. It was all so definite that I repeated the message to the woman verbatim and she accepted it. So here she was just now, calling back to say that they waited, the stone passed, and her daddy's just fine! Isn't that absolutely tremendous?"

Before any of us could comment, the phone rang again and

Olga rushed over to answer it. This time it was apparently someone from San Francisco and Olga's emphatic response to the caller was: "Look, honey, how can I help you when you don't even know what help you want? Why don't you get yourself a doctor and find out if you really are pregnant? That's right. Then when you know what's what for sure, let me know and we'll take it from there."

As Olga started back, she stopped suddenly and said, "I'm going to shut this phone off temporarily so we can get on with our discussion. It just never stops—as bad as any doctor's! Right, Edwina?"

"Worse even!" I agreed. "It rings like a general practitioner's line where he's the only M.D. in a one-horse town."

Olga laughed as she turned off the telephone. Then she sat down again and asked, "Where were we?"

It was Father Timothy who replied first. "You were explaining the 'psychic overlay' in your kind of spiritual healing," he said, "and frankly, it leaves me in a quandary. What I mean is: do I have to have some kind of psychic ability in order to do spiritual healing? Is that a prerequisite for setting up a healing service in a church, or for even attempting spiritual healing? Because I'm about as nonpsychic as you can get!"

"Definitely not," Olga reassured him. "The spiritual healing I do is enhanced by my psychic gift, but spiritual healing can be, and usually is, accomplished by people who are neither clairvoyant nor clairaudient, nor mediumistic in any way. The healing current flows through every clear channel available, whatever the healer's psychic abilities or, for that matter, religious beliefs. As a matter of fact, I don't profess to have psychic intervention available in every case. My clairvoyance is entirely spontaneous and can't be turned on and off at will. Many people call me and expect a prompt psychic diagnosis—as if their ten-cent pieces in the telephone should start my motor up like coins in a washing machine. Sometimes it does, and sometimes it doesn't."

Father Wellesly asked a question next: "Are you totally in favor of the churches, through their clergymen naturally, offering spiritual healing?"

"Absolutely." Olga was emphatic. "The New Life Clinic, which you attended this morning, is not only housed in the Methodist church, but is *accepted* by the Mount Washington Church as well. In the early days of Christianity, the so-called gifts of the spirit were practiced in the churches and healing was a vital one that was demonstrated and accepted. Good lord, what do you think Jesus was doing and preaching? He healed the sick wherever he went and he told his followers to 'go and do likewise.' A sincere minister, a dedicated doctor—people like these are often, without knowing it themselves, spiritual healers. They take a pulse, put an arm around a sufferer, and act as unconscious channels for God's healing energy."

Olga then went on to explain that the "laying-on of hands" is an important part of a neophyte spiritual healer's development. As for her own approach, however, distance healing was equally effective because of her educated awareness of the universal field of energy which surrounds both her and the patients who ask for help. In absent treatments, for example, Olga declared that she not only could feel a cool kind of power flowing from her solar-plexus, but often was cognizant of specific instruction and assistance from the spirit world in general or, at times, from one or more of several discarnate physicians in particular.

"But you do the 'laying-on of hands' at the healing clinic," Father Timothy said.

"Of course I do," Olga replied. "Actually, there are many ways of giving spiritual healing. When I sit in the 'silence' every night at nine o'clock and pray, I am using distance healing. When I go to the church every Thursday morning for the service, I do the 'laying-on of hands.'"

"What do you feel when you put your hands on someone?"

I asked. "Or don't you feel anything at all?"

Olga didn't have to grope for her response. "When I put my hands on a person," she said, "a heat seems to be generated from my hands. People say it feels like hot pads. Sometimes I experience a sensation, sort of like an electrical discharge, with a pins-and-needles pricking on my palms and fingertips. Here," she suddenly interrupted herself, "see how cool my hands are."

She held out her hands for us to feel and they were very ordinary, average-sized hands, neat, ringed, and entirely cool.

"Just watch," Olga continued, "I'm going to place my hands on Father Wellesly's back" (this was the first I heard of the minister's difficulty) "and you tell them, Father Wellesly, how do my hands feel now?"

"By jove!" he exclaimed in astonishment. "They're hot. They're really hot! Incredible!"

"Again," Olga warned us, "I want you to bear in mind that this doesn't happen in every single case. There are no guarantees or even sure-fire effects in spiritual healing. I don't shriek or chant or look up to the heavens in order to make the healing power start to flow. When conditions are right, it just does. It's completely impersonal. I am only a channel for this healing force that comes from God, but I have no control over it. I simply relax and let the strange power do the work. I believe it is of God, that it has intelligence far beyond my intelligence, even though I am part of that enlarged intelligence. In order for this power to do the necessary healing—and I want you to remember this, especially when you set up your own healing services in your own churches—one should be quiescent, peaceful, calm, relaxed, and expectant."

Father Wellesly was still excited by the heat that had emanated from Olga's hands when they were on his back. "I wouldn't have believed it," he exclaimed again, when she paused. "It was like diathermy heat—went down about one inch under my skin! Tell me, please: is the amount of heat generated a measurement of the healing that takes place?"

"I don't really know." Olga was obviously intent on stark, naked honesty. "Ambrose thinks it may well be so because heat stimulates motion in the atoms which make up the body. But that science stuff is beyond me."

"And another thing." Father Wellesly pursued his analysis with animation. "You placed your hands on me rather lightly, with no pressure at all. Is that how you always do the laying-on of hands?"

"Usually," Olga replied. "In fact, when I have my hands on a person, it feels as though there's a separation of maybe a quarter of an inch from me and the person, although I know for a certainty that I am touching him. It's sort of as if my spiritual body is slightly dissociated from my physical body when I'm in the healing situation. And not only just because of this lack of normal sensation of contact in my hands, but also because my body has no sense of weight whatsoever and no feeling of tiredness. How can I explain it? My body is there but it's almost like a shadow. Do you see? Do you get what I'm trying to say?"

Father Timothy nodded, somewhat hesitantly. Then he asked, while Father Wellesly and I wrestled silently with the whole idea: "Are you aware of anything else when you are healing? For example, Father Wellesly felt that heat from your hands. Did you?"

"Not this time," Olga said. "Many times, though, I do feel a tingling sensation coming out of my hands, almost electrical."

"Like the kind of shock you get when you touch an electric wire?" I asked.

"Oh no!" Olga was somewhat emphatic. "It's much more like a bunch of needle points pricking my fingers."

On and on the questions went and they were seemingly endless.

Could Olga tell when someone called or came to the church

service for healing, if healing would really be forthcoming for that person?

Apparently she could not, she never knew. Any healing is an experiment and any experiment, by virtue of its experimental nature, is not subject to guarantees.

Did Olga know for a certainty, once a healing treatment had been given, if a healing would take place?

Again, Olga disclaimed any such knowledge. Occasionally she might be told psychically that an individual would be entirely well or that a physical ailment would be cured. Usually, though, she holds a person in prayer and never even thinks, much less knows, whether the healing has been accomplished. The spiritual forces are unleashed, but they come from God and the work is done by him—not by her.

Does Olga regard prayer as a distinct element of her therapy?

This reply was most emphatic. Prayer on the part of a healer is a necessity: not the customary prayer of striving, petitioning, urging, or bargaining, but a request to be used as a healing channel and an expression of deep gratitude for the fulfillment of the request. Prayer on the part of the patient, however, is not an essential ingredient for successful spiritual healing.

This last remark evoked an immediate Why not?

"Because," Olga explained, seemingly amused but also tolerant of our shocked surprise, "the healing energy flows constantly from God. When it is channeled by the prayer of the spiritual healer, it 'falleth like the gentle rain from heaven' on good and bad alike; on those who ask, believing, and on those who can't or won't pray at all.

"Now mind you," she said earnestly, "prayer, especially affirming prayer, is a tremendous force field of healing action. The patient who can pray affirmatively is way up ahead. Sincere, deep faith can, on its own, activate the healing energy. What I *am* saying is that prayer on the part of the sick person who is seeking help is not an *essential* step in the spiritual healing process. It is a beneficial step, but not a prerequisite."

Father Wellesly posed the next question. "If prayer on the part of the sick person is not necessary," he asked thoughtfully, "is it because it is enough that he comes forward for healing? Is that what you mean?"

"Not even that," replied Olga. "A person comes forward in a healing service, of course, but in absent healing the sick often don't even know that someone else has asked me to help. She stood up and walked over to one of two tall, businesslike filing cabinets that stood on one side of the library. "Let me give you a for-instance," she said, opening a drawer and pulling out a paper. "Here's a letter from an army colonel in California. He phoned the first time about three weeks ago to ask me to hold his nineteen-year-old son in prayer. The boy was in a deep coma—had been for several weeks—as the result of an accident. I think he said it was a swimming-pool accident. But anyway, the point I'm making is that the boy was unconscious and certainly unable to ask me for help on his own. Nor could he pray—if he were the praying kind. Do you follow me? It's all there in the letter."

It was all there in the letter—and much more. The colonel wrote to thank Olga for her help. Within a few days after the absent treatment had been begun by her, his son started to respond. Soon, wrote the colonel, the boy was taking physical therapy and making tremendous progress toward a complete recovery—such tremendous progress, in fact, that the doctor on the case, the nurses at the hospital, and the physical therapist were excited and amazed. "Thank you from the bottom of my heart," wrote the grateful father. "What else can I say?"

Olga laughed when we commented on the contents of the letter. "Children," she declared, "those cabinets are stuffed full of letters like that. They come from every part of the world and from every kind of person. They thank me, but I thank God."

We looked at the cabinets and Father Wellesly asked the

question uppermost in my mind. "Look here," he said, "I don't mean to be bullish about this. I know you stated that you don't keep records. But on the basis of those communications in your files, what would you say your percentage of successful healings was?"

"Well," Olga answered slowly, "if you want to go on the basis of our files, I would say that roughly ninety percent of people we try to help are *improved*. As for actual complete cures—that's about fifty or so percent. And I'm making an educated guess."

Father Timothy looked rather wistful. "Do you really think I can bring spiritual healing to my parishioners?" he asked.

"God can," Olga spoke emphatically. "Even through you. Remember: you would be only a channel, but the healing energy of God is limitless. Do you think he could run out?" She suddenly stopped and burst out laughing. "Timmie," she said, "you remind me of an old lady who came to our healing service one morning, and I'll tell you now what I told her then. She rushed up to the altar rail, the first one there, frantically, and actually panting. 'Mrs. Worrall,' she breathed heavily, 'I hurried so to get here first. I wanted to be sure to be right in front of you before the power got all used up.' 'Honey,' I answered her, almost before I could think, 'how could God get all used up? His power is without end. But we take from that power according to what we bring to take with—be it a teaspoon or a bushel basket.' So Timmie," Olga finished, "get out your bushel basket."

With this as an introduction, she then launched into a detailed set of instructions for both the clergymen concerning the mechanics and principles involved in establishing healing services in a church. The discussion went on for a long time and I sat, for the most part, just listening.

At three o'clock Olga went out to the kitchen and came back with a silver tray laden with tea and cookies. At four o'clock she was still talking and answering questions and asking questions, but her voice sounded less vigorous and her face looked tired.

Watching her, I suddenly thought, "Good Lord! Here we are, three absolute strangers to her, barging in out of the nowhere, taking her time and her strength. What right do we have to impose? Why does she do it?"

Then I remembered the whole session in the church and I wondered even more. All of those people were strangers too, yet she had not only conducted the healing service for them, but had gone about afterward, listening to their stories, offering encouragement, and distributing advice. Why?

I got my chance to ask Olga this along about five o'clock. Father Wellesly had remembered a plane he had to catch a few minutes earlier and he and Father Timothy had left hurriedly amid a profusion of grateful acknowledgments from them and affectionate hugs from Olga. I stayed behind, briefly, to help Olga clear away the tea things and to put the notes I had taken that afternoon into some semblance of order before packing them.

"Olga," I began, "you must be tired."

"Nope," she responded, "why must I be?"

We both laughed. Then I went on more seriously. "What makes you drive yourself this way? I know you don't get a penny for what you do. So why do you do it? The clinic, the phone calls, the letters—the whole bit. Why?"

"Honey," Olga said, looking at me cheerfully over the china cup she was washing, "I've done this all my life—one way or another. Somehow, even when I was a very little girl back in Cleveland, we all sort of knew that there was some kind of healing in my hands. My mother would ask me to put my hands on her when something hurt her and I would be asked by the neighbors, too, to help. They were old-country Russians, you know, and they just accepted the fact that something good happened when I touched them."

She paused for a moment, remembering. Then she continued: "When I got older, and after I married Ambrose, I
came to see that we were meant to do this. Not at first, of
course. When we moved to Baltimore, I was determined to be
an ordinary housewife and Ambrose was going to be just an
engineer. No more clairvoyance or healing or anything odd!
Why, even when our babies were sick, it never occurred to us
to try to heal them. But afterward we both came to realize that
our gift of healing should be shared—freely and for free."

"How did you come to realize this?" I asked. "I mean, how
did you get back into healing?"

"You make it sound as if we suddenly decided to hang out
a shingle!" Olga laughed in reply. "Seriously though, it just sort
of happened. Somebody at work had heard from somebody in
the Martin office in Cleveland, where Ambrose used to work,
that Ambrose had done healing out there. He asked Ambrose
to help someone here. Well, one thing led to another and,
before too long, we were handling people in our house here
almost every night. It all just grew by word of mouth."

"And now," I concluded for her, "you don't see anyone here
anymore, but you run the New Life Clinic and go about lecturing and holding healing services everywhere, from Baltimore
to Japan, and responding to telephone requests until it still
takes just about your whole life. Why?"

"It *is* my whole life," Olga replied firmly. "I feel I have a
twofold mission: To spread spiritual healing whenever and
wherever I can; and to preach the gospel of survival, especially
to the bereaved, through my clairvoyance. These are the talents God has given me. They are his gifts to me and it is my
responsibility to use them fully."

Olga spoke solemnly and surely. Her eyes were shining as
if she were looking into a soft but bright light. She had expressed a dedication that few of us ever possess in regard to
anything. It was noble; it was inspirational; but it was not that

easy to accept; and I thought her words over inwardly as I collected my things and followed her out the house door and down the front path.

Suddenly, as we neared the street, we were stopped by a woman who apparently had been waiting there. She was forty-ish; her eyes were red and swollen; and she spoke frantically.

"Are you Mrs. Worrall?" She asked, grabbing my arm.

"I'm Mrs. Worrall," Olga answered, stepping forward. "Is there something you want?"

"Oh, Mrs. Worrall," the woman replied. "I've brought my son to you. He's right there in the car. Please, let me bring him in."

"I'm sorry," Olga said, "but I don't see anyone in my house anymore. Why don't you bring him to the New Life Clinic next Thursday?"

"But you don't understand!" exclaimed the woman. "It can't wait! He's shaking so. It's some kind of convulsion. He had some mild kind of a nervous breakdown and they put him on some drugs. But now he doesn't even know us anymore. He just sits on the back seat of the car, thrashing about uncontrollably. Please, Mrs. Worrall, won't you help him? He's my only child."

The woman did not cry aloud, but tears streamed silently down her face. She was joined at this point by her husband, who had apparently been waiting in the car with the boy. His voice trembled as he, too, asked Olga to see their son; and the two of them, standing there in such abject dispair, such terrible distress, made me want to weep also. Only Olga seemed able to maintain some degree of composure.

"Is he in this car?" she asked, moving briskly toward an old Chevrolet parked at the curb. "Now remember, I can't promise anything, but I will lay my hands on him and hold him in prayer that God may heal him. Help me open the door. It's locked."

The door was unlocked immediately and I stood beside Olga

as she bent down to reach inside. For just a brief moment she seemed to falter at the tragic sight before us: the twitching body, the bestial panting, the vacant stare of the fifteen-year-old boy who sat, half-crouched, on the back seat. Then she reached forward to try to place her hands on his jerking head, but he was shaking so much that it took several attempts before she could do so.

As Olga held her hands lightly in place, finally a gradual change was obvious to the three of us who stood by, tensely watching. Little by little—although actually in just a matter of moments—the shaking slowed until it almost stopped and the empty-looking eyes fixed themselves still uncomprehendingly, but wonderingly, on Olga's face.

In the awesome silence in which we all stood, scarcely daring to breathe aloud, I followed the boy's gaze and turned my head also to look upon Olga's face: it was pale in the fading daylight and it was drawn with unmistakable weariness. The lips quivered ever so slightly and the eyes were filled with unshed tears. Over the whole of it, though, and lighting it up as if there were a candle shining from deep down within, was an expression of deep compassion and love which illuminated even my stubborn soul.

Just like that, in a sudden glow of understanding, I realized the truth of what Olga Worrall had been teaching and demonstrating for us throughout that long day. She could not define spiritual healing, as she had indeed said in the beginning. She could only attempt to establish its validity by her honest practice of it and her specific results. The problem, then, was what one chose to make of these results.

For me, the answer to this question lay in Olga Worrall herself. I had seen her in the chapel, ministering to hundreds. I had watched her by the side of the road caring for the stranger. I had heard her on the telephone responding to countless requests. I could bear witness in fact to the sincerity, entirety, and dedication of what she called her "mission."

Granted that spiritual healing remained still an enigma to me. Granted that I was no nearer yet to understanding how or why anything happened when a spiritual healer undertook to heal. I knew only that at long last I found myself ready and willing to accept Olga Worrall's word for it that many wonderful, unexplainable things did happen.

CHAPTER V

Entering the Crystal Ball

Unlike spiritual healing, which admittedly requires a leap of faith, psychic phenomena present a credibility hurdle that comparatively few can surmount. Unseen presences that speak silently and spirit manifestations that "go bump in the night" all defy logic and reality. Despite the current growing awareness and parlor-game interest in the occult, there is little danger that the Ouija board will soon displace gin rummy. A basic disbelief prevails which either openly disputes or tolerantly ridicules or, at best, merely ignores that whole vast world of the psychic unknown—and it was into this last category that I fell.

Having embarked upon my Olga Worrall research, however (and having definitely by now committed myself to writing this book), it was no longer possible for me to sit back and look the other way. Perhaps as significant as anything else that had emerged during that long afternoon at Olga's house was her declaration of her self-alleged "twofold mission": to bring spiritual healing to those in need of it and to establish proof of human survival after death. Certainly I had listened with an open mind to Olga Worrall's dissertation on spiritual healing. Surely, therefore, I should listen as attentively to her analysis of the psychic evidence of immortality.

Unfortunately, though, this was, for me, a very difficult task.

Generations of scoffers lay behind me—including a mother who would literally have washed my mouth out with soap had she heard me even allude to a ghost. A lifetime of mild skepticism and total indifference lay all about me—making it almost impossible, initially, for me to discuss the subject seriously without feeling that I sounded like a mental patient who argues out loud with people who aren't there or who dodges nonexistent knives which presumably fly at him through the empty air.

"Your mental block is not unusual," Olga reassured me in our subsequent talks. "Most people react as you do to the whole psychic bit. I've lived with that reaction ever since I was a little girl. My own parents were upset and often angry at my clairvoyance, and many times I wished I couldn't see things that no one else could see. I just yearned to be an ordinary person! But now I have long since made my peace with my gift and it's just part of me. But for you, this whole idea is so strange, it's almost crazy. You never even thought about any of this before, much less talked about it. So why shouldn't it shake you?"

Her sincere understanding and wholehearted acceptance of my attitude became the basic rock upon which my eventual investigation was built. When I said wistfully to her, "If I only could see one teeny-weeny ghost myself!" she merely laughed and replied, "'I never promised you a rose garden,' did I? or a visible ghost!" When I complained to her one day that I had never had the least type of parapsychological experience—not a precognizant dream, not a reliable forewarning hunch of any kind, not a single "I-have-been-here-before," deja vu kind of encounter, she only laughed some more.

"Honey," she said, "none of that would really make any difference. People who have experiences of that kind usually just rationalize them away anyway. They blame them on imagination, coincidence, or maybe even indigestion. Look at how Jesus went around performing miracles; how many saw them, but how comparatively few believed! So please: stop batting yourself over the head about this psychic stuff. Since it even embarrasses you just to talk about it, let's not. When the time is ripe and you're ready to listen to what I have to say —not to believe, mind you, but just to listen!—then come along and we'll talk. Okay?"

Amazingly enough, at least to me, the time did come, and soon; although in a completely unexpected way. We were at a dinner party one evening with a group of doctor friends when the subject of Olga Worrall and her spiritual healing came up as a result of an article that had appeared about her in *Medical Economics.*

"I don't know what to think," one of the doctors said. "According to this piece I read in *Medical Economics,* this woman achieves results where orthodox medicine has failed. They say doctors not only refer patients to her but seek her out for themselves. It certainly sounds incredible!"

I sat almost motionless, maintaining a careful silence, reluctant to be a name-dropper by saying, "I know her" and still more reluctant to reveal my involvement via my whole project. Then another doctor added his commentary on the piece, which he had also skimmed, and I just had to respond.

"It is totally incredible," the second doctor said. "*They* say she doesn't accept one cent for what she does—which I certainly don't believe—and *she* says that what she does is spiritual healing—which makes me think she must be just another kook."

"She's not a kook!" Without any further thought, I launched into a brief description of what Olga Worrall did, what she maintained, and what she was like.

By the time I had finished speaking and answering several pertinent questions, I had clarified for myself, as well as for those present, my personal conviction concerning Olga's integrity. I thought about it further after I got home and there was still no doubt in my mind. Olga Worrall was honest and frank. There was nothing phony about her. She was also definitely intelligent, with a kind of earthy, salty common sense that delightfully flavored an otherwise surprising measure of intellectuality. Her practical approach to life and her spontaneous humor made her an endless source of sound and witty advice that put Dear Abby into the realm of a mid-Victorian, lovelorn columnist. Her warmth and human compassion were as genuine and spectacular as the Hope Diamond—and I realized suddenly and fully, as I added it all up, how much I had come to respect and to trust Olga Worrall.

The corollary to this realization was immediately forthcoming. If you trust and respect someone, and if this trusted and respected someone tells you something you know nothing about, but that seems utterly outlandish, do you turn away and refuse to hear him out? Don't you, on the basis of respect and trust alone, suspend judgment until you at least listen?

Reducing this logic to its simplest, specific terms meant that I should start listening to Olga Worrall's psychic history, whatever my personal conceptions or misconceptions were about the subject. It was a somewhat reluctant conclusion, however, that was fortunately bolstered a few days later by another unexpected event which ended any further hesitation.

The morning after the dinner party, I received a telephone call from a physician whom we knew quite well but who had not been present at the discussion the night before. In fact, as I answered the phone, I realized all at once that we hadn't heard from Arnold for at least six months. After the usual opening amenities, I learned why.

"Edwina," he said in a strained-sounding voice, "I met George Pearson in the hospital staff room today. He was telling me about you-all getting together last night and he happened to mention that you know that Worrall woman who was written up in *Medical Economics*. Is that right?"

"That's right," I answered cautiously.

"Good." He seemed to breathe a sigh of relief. "Look here, let me tell you why I called. Have you heard about Keith?"

Keith was Arnold's oldest child and only son. About twenty-six, I remembered; over six feet tall; robust looking with a big, ready grin; and a senior in law school. The facts flipped rapidly through my mind, like figures rolling out of a computer, while I answered: "What haven't I heard about Keith?"

"He's got H.D., Hodgkins disease." For a moment Arnold didn't seem able to say anything more and I breathed a shocked, "God no!" Then he continued. "He came down with what we all thought was infectious mononucleosis about eight months ago. When it didn't clear properly, we began doing more and more tests. At first the results were negative or questionable, but pretty soon the diagnosis became indisputable. His spleen has been removed and he's been carefully staged for the disease and he's even had chemotherapy, but he still complains of pains. Edwina," he finished, "we're practically out of our minds. We pray and pray and we're ready to try anything. If that *Medical Economics* article is straight, then we want Keith to go see that Worrall woman. Can you arrange it?"

"I can try," I responded promptly. "You do remember, though, that even in the story about her, it stated that she doesn't see anyone in her home anymore. And I know that that's true. But I will try."

"Thanks." His voice was husky. "Just tell us when and we'll be there."

We talked for a while longer, and in response to my questions, he filled me in more fully on the whole situation. Then I hung up and called Olga.

Her initial response was as I had expected: "Tell him to come to the New Life Clinic any Thursday morning."

"But Olga," I answered, "you don't understand. I know this family well. They're devout Catholics. They've tried everything. Now just listen to me before you say No."

Olga listened. After a few sentences, she interrupted me and said, "Honey, you win. Bring them here next Saturday evening at seven o'clock. See you all then."

She hung up before I could ask, "Why me?" Instead, I called Arnold back and we arranged to drive over together at the appointed time. He would have Keith in the car and he would pick me up, too.

"I didn't really plan to go along," I told Arnold apologetically, "but she seemed to just assume it. Do you mind?"

"Of course not," he said, and I could tell he meant that.

On Saturday evening, therefore, our delegation arrived at Olga Worrall's. She met us at the front door with her usual gracious manner and she insisted, after my brief introductions, that we sit around in her living room and "get acquainted." Mostly, this meant that Olga asked Arnold what he, as a medical doctor, knew about spiritual healing—which was nothing —and that Arnold asked Olga, as the subject of the *Medical Economics* article which had brought him and his son to her doorstep, what she thought of the accuracy of the piece. When it had been adequately established that Arnold believed in God and the possibility of a healing power that emanated from God, and that Olga considered the article to be substantially correct and a fair portrayal of spiritual healing, she finally said: "Why don't we go upstairs to the healing room and get down to business." Then, as only Keith got up to follow her, she added, "Come on, doctor, and see what spiritual healing is for yourself. And you, too, Edwina. I know you're curious as always."

I was curious about the "healing room" which I had heard about but never seen—and I examined it with great interest as we entered. Actually, it was just a bedroom originally, but its conversion into a spiritual treatment center was complete. There were red brocade draperies hanging at the sides of the two windows and a red oriental rug on the floor; there was a small table with a lamp on it, a narrow sofa on one side, an upholstered chair, two straight-backed chairs and an armless, padded couch in the center of the room on which a patient could lie down. The walls were especially interesting with a striking etching of Jesus and an enlarged photograph of a handsome young man, surrounded overhead by a group of bodiless faces.

"That's Ambrose," Olga explained, as she noticed my inter-est in the picture. "Way back in his youth. A photographer friend of his took that and nearly fainted when the negative was developed and revealed a row of spirit faces too. It was a complete surprise to both of them—but that does happen sometimes. Ambrose got some like that on his own, also. One, in particular, occurred years ago. He snapped his two sisters and when the print came back, there was a spirit child on it also."

By now, we were all seated and Olga asked cheerfully: "Are you comfortable? I enjoy comfort," she laughed. "To me, all things beautiful, as well as good, are part of the fullness of life that God wants for us. Obviously, if you go haywire over material possessions, that's enslavement and wrong. But just show me where the Ten Commandments say, 'Thou shalt be poor.' Nope! Even Jesus' friend Lazarus, whom he raised from the dead, was rich—and Jesus himself wore a 'seamless robe' —the one the soldiers cast lots for—and a semaless robe was the most expensive garment you could get in those days.

"But enough of this talk," Olga interrupted herself. "Keith, you come here."

At her bidding, Keith lay down on the armless couch and Olga proceeded to ask him specific questions about his general condition and how he felt. She touched different parts of his body where she said she knew—clairvoyantly—that he had some pain. Then she had him sit down on one of the straight-beacked chairs so she could give him what she called a charge of healing spiritual energy.

While this was going on, Arnold and I were sitting on opposite sides of the room. Because of this positioning, when Olga placed her hands on Keith's upper abdominal area, her back was turned to Arnold, but both she and Keith were clearly within my view—in fact, just about four or five feet away from me, and in bright lighting.

I watched intently as Olga's hands rested on Keith's body, one hand in front and the other on his back. As she stood thus, in absolute silence and with her eyes gently closed, I suddenly became aware of an almost colorless, thin kind of vapory stuff that floated like smoke from the absolutely nonexistent space between Olga's hand and Keith's body. What on earth could this be? I blinked my eyes, as if to clear the air, but it was still there. I stared unbelievingly until Olga lifted her hand away from Keith—and the whatever-it-was immediately disappeared.

"Olga," I exclaimed, "I must be hallucinating—or something. I just can't believe my own eyes! When you had your hand on Keith, I saw something emerging!"

Olga was delighted, but not terribly surprised. "Did you really see it, Edwina?" She asked. "I've seen that many times when Ambrose was doing the laying-on-of-hands, but of course I've never watched myself. It's an ectoplasmic mist and it can be seen emanating from a healer's hands when he's healing—sometimes."

"Ectoplasmic mist!" I repeated wonderingly. "Good heavens!—That's sort of a spiritual manifestation, isn't it?"

"I couldn't even see Mrs. Worrall's hands from where I sat," Arnold said, with obvious disappointment.

"Well, I saw it," I declared, "but I still can't believe it."

"But what does it mean?" Keith asked. "Does it have any significance as to healing?"

Olga laughed in reply. "If you mean, is it a guarantee of success," she said, "then the answer is No. Actually, that kind of ectoplasmic transfer is present in all spiritual healing, except that it's usually not visible. When it is visualized with the naked eye—as Edwina did today—it simply stands as a kind of demonstration of the fact that something really happens when a healer puts his hands on a recipient. You might call it proof, in a way, that the unexplainable does exist even when we can't see it or understand it. But even so, it's proof only if someone is ready to accept it."

At that point, finally, I was. Within a few days, therefore, I was back at Olga Worrall's house, freed from any further hesitation and asking question after question about the paranormal.

"If someone like me could see something as unbelievable as that smoky kind of vapor coming out of nowhere," I told Olga as we began to talk, "then maybe there are many other things that I can't see that someone like you can."

"I can," Olga replied firmly, launching into an opening statement. "Not as a parlor trick and not for hire. I'm fully aware that to most people, anyone who not only professes belief in a spirit world but who goes so far as to communicate with it, belongs in a booby hatch. The only reason that I have been willing to make my psychic experiences public has been my feeling of responsibility that this gift of mine must be used to help people. As I told you before, one of my life-missions is to provide proof and increase the acceptance of human survival after death."

"But how does your psychic gift do that?" I asked, needing my usual Seeing-Eye-dog assistance before I could make any connections in this strange new territory.

"Honey," Olga explained patiently, "when I transmit a

highly evidential message from a spirit to a loved one he has left behind, that's proof. Even the most skeptical have to stop and think: 'Where did she get this information that only Cousin Harry or Aunt Mary knew; and how could she get it from him or from her unless, in some form, in some way, Cousin Harry or Aunt Mary had told her; and how could they have told her if they were not alive?' Do you see?"

"But don't people often say that's just ESP?" I asked.

"Just ESP?" Olga laughed. "That's no 'just.' Getting some of these diehard atheists to enlarge their materialistic notions of the world so that they have to give credit to something as intangible as extrasensory perception is a great step forward in itself. Besides, mostly they call it ESP as a kind of rationalization, but they really don't know what to think. Believe me, they may disclaim it but it shakes them up."

I could see that. It had shaken me up, too.

"Here's a perfect example," Olga went on. "Remember, when I was down in Virginia several weeks ago at that Blue Ridge College conference? Well, a reporter was interviewing me at dinner and suddenly, while I was talking to him, I saw an older woman, his mother, standing beside him—clairvoyantly, that is. I described her to him in detail and repeated what she was telling me to tell him. Specifically, she wanted him to know that, although she hated to leave him, she was very happy. His father had met her when she went over and so had his sister. Also, she asked him particularly to stop grieving so much for his aunt who had come over a few weeks ago, because she, too, was with them. There were other facts and instructions given, and when I had finished, the reporter burst into tears and had to leave the room. He returned after a while to thank me for the messages and to tell me that I had described his mother accurately; that she had died three months ago; that they had been very close; that his father and sister had passed on before; that his very much beloved aunt had

died only a few weeks previously and that he had been incon-
solable after this last loss. He told me, 'You've given me new
hope. I thought everything was over and done with, but now
I feel that I may see them all again some day.'" Olga smiled,
remembering. "Isn't that beautiful?" she asked.

I nodded in reply. Then I spoke my thoughts aloud. "Proof
of survival does give hope, and hope gives strength to the
bereaved. I sometimes think that, as much as anything Jesus
did, his demonstration of his continued existence, his resurrection, his reappearance to his followers—this was his greatest
lesson of all."

"Exactly!" Olga's face beamed. "The burning question for
all mankind has always been: 'If a man die, shall he live again?'
And Jesus *showed* us—not told us—but showed us that the
answer is Yes. No other religious leader actually came back to
demonstrate the continuity and immortality of human existence as he did. Because it was so important to him in his
ministry, I feel it should be important to me to use my psychic
gifts to this effect. To prove human survival beyond the grave
is not only to encourage and console those who mourn, but to
give meaning and purpose to all who live; it is to teach what
to expect in the hereafter so that a ready and easy adjustment
can be made when the time for passing-on comes."

Again I nodded in agreement. Then I asked, not baitingly
but earnestly: "Olga, do you really believe that you know what
to expect in the so-called hereafter?"

"Honey," she answered, even more earnestly, "I've been
there. I know."

"But how?" I was obviously startled.

"I've traveled in the astral," she said. "I've talked with spirits, also, who've told me many things. I can see you gaping, so
let me explain.

"Man," said Olga, "is spirit. On earth he has a spiritual body
encased in a body of flesh. He operates primarily through the
spiritual body; the physical body merely responds to his or-

ders, producing effects on the physical level, and carrying sensation back to the spiritual body from the physical world. We are therefore living in the spiritual world even while encased in flesh, but our attention is so strongly concentrated on what is happening on the physical level that we are virtually oblivious to the activities on the spiritual level.

"During the time when the physical body is unconscious, as in sleep, the spiritual body takes a temporary leave of absence. It can stay in the immediate vicinity of the physical body or it can travel vast distances. It goes where it wants to go, it does what it wants to do, under the direction of the individual. Thus you will find the spirit of the miser guarding his treasure while his body sleeps; the spirit of the musician seeks the more nearly perfect interpretation of his favorite composition; the humanitarian finds more effective ways to serve; and the philosopher seeks wisdom that he might satisfy the needs of his students.

"We should give much thought to that portion of our life's span that is the sum total of our unconscious existence on earth. It amounts to about twenty-five years of earth time. We should use it wisely, for during this quarter of a century of sleep we can be gathering a vast knowledge of our life as it is lived in the world beyond, and reflect this in our mode of life on earth."

"Is that what you mean by traveling astrally?" I asked Olga when she paused for breath.

"Yes," she said. "Not every night, of course, but many nights when I go to sleep, I leave my physical body behind and go off in my astral or spiritual body. Most people don't recall what takes place during their sleep, but whenever I've made an astral trip, I remember it and know it for what it is the next day."

I was still puzzled. "But how can you be sure that you haven't just had a vivid dream?"

"First, because I simply am conscious of what happens,"

Olga answered. "Then, too, because I've had verification of some of my astral visits. Obviously, when I've been to the spiritual realm, there's only my word for it, but on other more mundane travels, I have seen people and circumstances that were substantiated later. For example: one night, I found myself leaving my physical body asleep on my bed and going to Cleveland. My mother was in the kitchen ironing—even though it was late at night—and one of my brothers was most unexpectedly there also, talking to her. I saw them and heard them but they couldn't see me or hear me. Finally I left, and the next day I wrote my mother, told her nothing, but just asked where she had been that night at the specified time, with whom, and what had been said. Her return letter confirmed everything I had noted during my astral visit, including her comment to my brother: 'I have such a strong, sudden feeling of Olga. I hope she's all right.'"

While I sat thinking this one over, Olga came up with an even more amazing illustration. "Here's a still more impressive example," she said, remembering it with mounting excitement, "and it's one Ambrose and I shared. He was in the midwest on a business trip, some years ago, and I was home alone. That night, after we had both gone to bed in our different cities, Ambrose found himself back in our home in Baltimore. He went upstairs and saw the bathroom light I had left on because I was alone. He didn't realize he was in the astral until he tried to turn it off and his hand went right through the switch. So he came to the bed and I awoke and saw him standing there. 'Get up and turn off the bathroom light,' he kept impressing on my mind telepathically. As I got the message and arose, he disappeared. Realizing that this had not been a mere physical visit, I wrote it all down. When he returned the next day, I had him write his account separately, and when we compared notes, they tallied perfectly."

As she finished speaking, Olga sighed. "Honey," she said, "I could give you incident after incident of astral travel that has been verified. I visited Ambrose's boyhood home in England years before we ever went there and wrote out a complete description of the old house, including a most unusual kind of stairway I could never in my life have imagined. But what's the use? Most people are so earthbound, they never dare take off astrally even though they are able to do it."

"But the idea is so fascinating!" I exclaimed. "Do you still have any of the writings in which you recorded these happenings?"

Olga laughed. "I save everything," she said. "Sure I've got those notes—right here in these old files. I'll get your proof."

She stood up and flipped through one of the filing cabinets in the library where, as usual, we were sitting. In just a few moments, she produced a batch of papers, some of which were yellowed with age.

"Take your time in looking them over," she advised. "I'll just go in the kitchen while you do and get us some lemonade. All this talk gets my throat dry."

I took my time. For quite a while after Olga returned with the lemonade, I sat in the quiet room reading the handwritten histories of the strange events she had told me about—plus some equally startling ones that she had not mentioned. Finally I finished my careful perusal and looked up at Olga.

"I honestly don't know what to make of all this," I said wonderingly.

"Who does?" asked Olga. "In fact, who knows what is or isn't real? Maybe reality lies in our dreaming, astral world altogether and we are really in a dream-state when we're awake. How can we be absolutely sure of anything?

"We believe that materialism has a firm foundation, but many scientists today have come to realize that their investigations carry them across the solid frontier into a realm beyond the limitations of matter. Certainly the religious world has long overstepped those boundaries. Some day, I am sure, science will catch up with belief—but, in the meantime, should I and people like me be silent? Do we not have a duty to speak out and satisfy the hunger in the human heart—even if it means the danger of being labeled nutty or deluded ourselves?"

How well I knew what Olga meant! There is an insatiable desire in almost every one of us, as well as a driving need and a deeply rooted fear, to know what comes after death. We stand beside the grave of a loved one and cry out silently that this cannot be all. We walk in the valley of the shadow many times during the course of a lifetime and quake inwardly at what might come next. We peer yearningly, fearfully into the vast unknown which constantly surrounds us, but we can neither penetrate it nor turn away.

"It is indeed the greatest, burning question for all mankind." Olga's reply once again to my unspoken thoughts no longer surprised me. "Come on, Edwina, drink up and I'll tell you what I know you're just curious as all get-out to know: what my astral travels and the spirit world have shown me of the beyond."

As usual, she was right. My curiosity was boundless. Obviously, Olga Worrall's description of what happens after death would not be subject to proof. As, obviously, the very premises upon which her entire presentation was based—the astral travel, the spirit entity of man, the psychic communication between the two worlds—were all equally nebulous and disputable.

Still, she thought she had answers and I knew I had none. Slowly but surely she had led me to the water, and I had decided for myself to drink.

CHAPTER VI

In My Father's House

Aᴀ BELIEF in immortality, to a greater or lesser extent, un-
derlies most of the world's religions. From the ancestor worship of the Shintoists to the Christian promise of "many mansions," human thought has been generally conditioned to the
idea of a hereafter. What is surprising, therefore, in view of the
prevalence of the overall principle, is the indignation and
ridicule which so often are heaped upon any serious attempt
to explore or even just to speculate on the specifics of what
that hereafter is all about.

Olga Worrall pointed out this pattern of inconsistent behav-
ior to me when we first began to delve into her version of life
after death. "Perhaps the problem stems from the traditional
heaven and hell business on which so many of us are raised,"
she commented. "That gets to be unpalatable after a while—
sort of too pat a solution, too clearcut—so we just shove the
whole survival bit into some dark corner of our minds and
rarely think about any of it until we come face to face with
death ourselves, or else lose somebody close to us."

"I know exactly what you mean," I agreed quickly. "Anything related to death or survival makes us extremely uneasy.
Lawyers say that's why so many people never make wills,
although advised to do so. But I'm over that hump now—and
while I'm not prepared as yet fully to credit or to accept what

you might say, I am intrigued with the possibility that you may really know what it's all about."

"I don't profess to know what it's all about," Olga corrected me. "I have learned only *some* of what happens. But first," she cautioned me next, "let me remind you that when you venture forth into Life After Death, you are literally and figuratively going off into thin air. Astral travel has an earthly base: you leave your physical body but you return to it also. Besides, there can be some verifications, as I mentioned before. The spirit world—that's even more intangible all the way. Tell me, Edwina," she finished laughingly, "how good are you at cloud-walking?"

"Well," I responded thoughtfully, "I've never tried it. Where should we begin?"

"You ask the questions," Olga countered, "and I'll answer all I can. If I don't know something, I'll tell you so. How's that?"

"Fair enough." I sat silent for a few moments after this response and finally said: "Why don't we start with death? That is, dying itself. Everybody dies, just as everyone gets born. From your psychic experience, what is dying like?"

According to Olga, dying is really birth, into the spirit world. It occurs when the body of flesh is no longer useful to the spirit. The spirit leaves the body in exactly the same way as when the body passes into the sleep state each night. Normally the spirit returns to and reenters the physical body after each period of sleep, just as described in astral or out-of-body travel. In death, the so-called silver cord, by which the spiritual body and physical body are joined to each other, is severed. When this detachment occurs, the spiritual body cannot reenter the physical body again.

"Death," said Olga, "is actually as painless as sleep. Disease may bring pain but death eliminates it. Death is no more to be feared than sleep, which most of us welcome. Did you ever read the statement on dying made by Sir William Osler, the famous physician?"

I shook my head no.

"He said," Olga repeated from memory, "that 'Most human beings not only die like heroes, but in my wide clinical experience, die really without pain or fear. There is as much oblivion about the last hours as about the first, and therefore, men fill their minds with specters that have no reality.'" Olga paused, then continued. "He obviously sensed from watching people die what I have learned as fact from the spirit world."

"Have you any idea of what dying is supposed to feel like?" I asked.

She had.

If consciousness is not lost as the spirit leaves the body for the last time, one may experience the pleasant process of the change. A lightness and feeling of peace is felt as the spirit slowly leaves the body. Then there is a sensation of floating as the spirit adjusts itself and stands apart from the body, which can be seen by the departing spirit. The room and all persons present are visible and the departing spirit will hear their comments. Should there be weeping the spirit will try to assure the mourners that he is well and alive, but in most cases they will not hear him because they have not developed the gift of clairaudience.

Gradually the scene takes on a misty experience as the spirit slowly retunes its consciousness from the world of the flesh to the world of the spirit. This may take the better part of an hour, after which the departing soul becomes slowly conscious of the new realm in which it will live, and the earth no longer seems real.

There is always someone waiting to greet a new soul entering the world of spirits. It may be a loved one, a close friend or simply someone who has been appointed to show him the way. Those who do not believe in life after death are quite confused when they find themselves in conscious existence after death. Many of them refuse to believe that they are among the so-called dead because the spirit world is so real to them in their new state of consciousness. It is only after meeting many other departed souls whom they knew to be dead that they begin to realize they are indeed in the new dimension.

"You cannot imagine," Olga declared, "the terrible state of mind in which people exist when they pass over without any knowledge of what to expect and can't understand or adjust to what is happening to them."

"What exactly do you mean?" I asked. "How can not knowing what to expect cause difficulty?"

"Well," Olga explained, "look at it from this point of view: the more narrow-visioned religionist, who expects to meet only those of his own creed in the other world, will upon arrival think that he has been denied admission to his conception of heaven because he will find himself associated with those he had been assured were on the wrong path, being of a different faith. Can you just picture his consternation? All of his earth life he had lived in fear of hell and eternal damnation. Why, it sometimes takes years to reeducate an enslaved mind! As a matter of fact, many who depart this earth life with such fixed misconceptions are so disturbed at the latitude that exists on the spirit plane that they must be placed in rest homes and treated until they are healed from the effects of their previous doctrines. And many of them respond only when those who have taught them their beliefs are assigned to these rest homes to reinstruct them in accordance with the truth that these instructors have come to learn themselves since their own passing."

I looked at Olga as she spoke and marveled at her certainty. She recited her piece the way Einstein must have originally presented his Theory of Relativity: deftly, definitely, and apparently unmoved, although completely aware of the skepticism with which his revolutionary new concept was being received.

"How can you be so sure of what you're saying?" I asked finally. "How can you know?"

"Honey," Olga reminded me, "I've visited some of those rest homes in the astral. What's more, both Ambrose and I have been called upon several times to help a newly arrived soul that was having trouble making an adjustment. This happens, incidentally, where there has been a sudden, unexpected passing—like someone killed in a war or in an accident."

"That would be a shockingly abrupt transition," I conceded. "Alive one moment, dead the next and then, if what you think is so, alive again, but in a different way."

"Exactly," she replied. "Now add to that the handicap of having no knowledge of the hereafter: it's shattering!"

"And you say," I pursued the subject further, "that you and Ambrose have, on occasion, helped these bewildered people?"

"We have." There was no doubt in Olga's voice. "Sometimes I don't remember very much and have only a faint recollection of what has taken place. That's when it happens in the astral and I recall things afterward as if it were a dream. Sometimes, though, I know exactly what's what—and can repeat it word by word."

"Can you tell me one such offhand?" I asked expectantly.

Olga thought for a few seconds, then she began: "Here's one I'll never forget. It occurred a number of years ago—again on one of those many nights when Ambrose had gone out of town on business and I was home alone. I had spent the evening reading the funnies and the rest of the paper until about eleven o'clock when I went to bed and promptly fell asleep. Almost immediately, however, I had what seemed at first to be a dream—except that I was positive that I was out of my body. A man, dressed all in white and with a brilliant light about him, took me by the hand and said, 'Come, my child, we have need of your help.'

"Because it seemed the thing for me to do and because he seemed so sure of my response, I followed him. In an instant, I found myself in the old Russian Orthodox church I had attended back in my childhood. There in the completely empty church was the priest I used to know and who had known me from the day I had been born. He looked very old as I approached him, and agitated—and I suddenly realized that I had not seen or heard from him for roughly seventeen or more years.

"How he recognized me, I do not know, but he called me by name. Then I took him by the hand—almost in response to some telepathic direction—and led him to the altar, which appeared to be dark although I could hear some indecipherable voices coming from within it. When we got to the altar, I stopped, as if somehow I knew I wasn't permitted to enter. He, however, was supposed to enter and I told him so, assuring him that, when he did, the men within it would help him along. The moment he stepped over the threshold of the altar, the whole altar was filled with a blazing, blinding white light. At the same time, the three men waiting there, all dressed in the beautifully colored robes of the priesthood, came forward, put their arms around him, and welcomed him in.

"Well, I thought, so that was my mission! Thinking it completed, therefore, I turned and walked out of the church. On the steps of the church, however, the figure in white that had directed me originally, stopped me again and informed me that I had more work to do. Before I could ask what next, I noticed the priest's wife walking up and down in front of the steps. She was older looking than I remembered and almost in a state of shock. When she caught sight of me, she knew me at once and began to cry, calling me by my childhood name: 'Olguska, Olguska dear! Help me, please, help me! I'm lost and so afraid! What has happened?'

"I stood with my arms around her, murmuring assurance

that she would be well taken care of and that she need never-
more be afraid. As I said this, I could sense that we were both
being gently lifted in the air and immediately set down on
what seemed to be a lovely country road lined on each side
with trees. There were a few cottages behind the trees and a
small group of men, women, and children heading toward us
on the road, singing as they came. As they drew near, the
priest's wife let go of my hand and cried out, as if overcome
with emotion: 'Mama! Papa!' In turn, her parents ran to her
and began to kiss and embrace her, while others crowded
about, greeting her lovingly, and several of the children scattered flower petals at her feet from baskets which they carried
on their arms.

"As she was being led away from me, she turned and waved
goodbye to me, thanked me, and threw me a kiss—and at this
point I once again knew telepathically that I had fulfilled a
given task. This was confirmed by the figure in white who
joined me as I turned away. He expressed his gratitude for my
assistance, promised me that all would now go well with the
priest and his wife—and I was back in my body in my own bed
in Baltimore!

"This awakening occurred before dawn, more or less in the
middle of the night, but I could sleep no more. Was it a dream?
Was it real? I hadn't even thought of those people for years!
What was it all about?

"The next morning I wrote down what had happened so as
to share it better with Ambrose when he returned. Then I
went into town on business and, when ready to return, obeyed
a strange compulsion to buy a newspaper that we never ordinarily read, although I knew our regular newspaper would
be waiting on my front porch when I got there.

"After I arrived home, one glance at the newspaper I had
purchased clarified everything. Right on the front page was a
small article which stated that the Reverend——and his wife,

of Cleveland, Ohio, had been killed instantly in an accident the day before, as they had been on their way to church. No other details were given and I hurriedly checked the newspaper that we had delivered every day, but it contained no mention at all of the accident. Further information was obtained from my family in Cleveland and this merely confirmed the accident which took the lives of those two old people I had been with the night before."

At this point in her story, Olga paused. "What a fascinating experience!" I couldn't help exclaiming. "And you feel that you were actually helping those people make an adjustment to their passing?"

"What else?" Olga commented drily. "Apparently the priest and his wife had died so unexpectedly and had been thrown out of their physical bodies with such force that they were earthbound and needed help. I don't know why I was chosen —unless it was felt that they needed someone whom they knew to be still living to show them the way."

The ringing of the telephone interrupted her just then, and when she returned in a few minutes, I was ready with my next question.

"Olga," I asked, "have you or Ambrose ever helped somebody make an adjustment when you were not in an out-of-body state? Have you ever dealt consciously with someone in spirit?"

Olga laughed. "Edwina," she said, "you should have been a public prosecutor! The answer is Yes. Let me see . . . oh yes, here's something that happened to Ambrose a number of years ago. And by the way, these experiences have been reduced to writing and have been corroborated by people who were around at the time."

She was silent briefly, as if in the process of remembering, and then began. "One night Ambrose was at the Martin plant, staying late because a number of his men were going to work overtime. He was alone for a while during the hour when the crew had gone out to get some dinner; including one young man—let's call him Jack—who decided to go home for his bite to eat since he lived just a few blocks away across the railroad tracks.

"As the men returned, Ambrose looked up and noticed that something about Jack seemed strange. He sat at his work-bench but he looked obviously bewildered. When he talked to somebody near him, there was no response. When he tried to pick up a tool, he couldn't because his hand went through it. Suddenly Ambrose realized that Jack was not Jack as he usually was; he was in spirit. But why? He had been well and alive only one hour before!

"Ambrose called Jack telepathically to come to him because he knew that no one else in the room could see Jack. The poor man came near, half in tears, and Ambrose tried to find out what had happened. It was immediately apparent that Jack didn't know; that he was terribly disturbed at being ignored by his co-workers; and that he sensed that something was wrong but couldn't understand what.

"When Ambrose attempted to explain to Jack that in the interval between leaving and returning to work something had ended his life, Jack protested wildly. It was ridiculous, it couldn't be! When Ambrose realized that he himself was not getting through to Jack or fully convincing him of the fact of his death, Ambrose asked the help of specific spirit entities with whom he had previously worked, to take Jack in hand and lead him away.

"Then Ambrose turned to the men who were busy with their jobs. He told them that Jack had been fatally injured and he sent one of them out to find out what had happened. In just a few minutes, the verification was brought back: Jack had been hurrying to the plant after having had a quick meal at home. He had been crossing the railroad tracks, somehow unaware of an oncoming train which unfortunately hit him and killed him instantly."

Before I could comment on this account, the telephone rang again. This time when Olga returned from answering it, she said, "Honey, I'm going to have to go out now. How about a return engagement tomorrow?"

"Fine," I agreed promptly. "Just answer one more question while I collect my things. I understand from what you said that there are spirit entities waiting to assist new arrivals in the spirit world to make an adjustment. Why, then, didn't they stand by to help Jack—or your priest and his wife?"

Olga followed me to the door as she answered. "They were standing by," she said, "but because of the swift and sudden deaths involved in these cases, the passing souls were still so earthbound that they couldn't quite see the hovering spirits. They could be more easily reached and persuaded by mediumistic people, like Ambrose or me, who were still alive and whom the frightened and confused newly departed knew were still alive. It's this earthbound state, incidentally, that is responsible for so-called hauntings which sometimes follow violent and unexpected deaths."

"I see." I replied automatically, almost absentmindedly, my thought processes still reeling from such total immersion in this whole strange philosophy and its particularized jargon: earthbound; spirit entities; hauntings; sudden passings. What did it really mean? How could I know?

In a way I was almost pleased to terminate our discussion for the day so that I could go home and mull over everything. Not that mulling over everything would really do any good. We had come so very far from the tangible, physical world in our talks by this stage that I felt as if I had somehow been removed to a different plane, way beyond any landmarks of reality— and a single night's sleep, obviously, could do nothing (and indeed did do nothing!) to resolve my mental turmoil.

Nevertheless, I was definitely hooked. Whether I understood or misunderstood, whether I believed or disbelieved, I wanted to hear whatever else Olga Worrall could tell me about her version of life after death. Accordingly, there I was the next day—and many following days, too—carefully pursuing the intriguing and utterly incredible subject.

Olga described the world beyond death as a purely spiritual world, which she further defined as an entirely mental world. In her own words: "Because of this aspect of life after death, we see and experience things with which we are attuned. Those who are strongly materialistic will find themselves associating the limiting laws of the physical universe with the spirit world, and they will be unable to take full advantage of the much greater freedom available in that realm. Their conceptions of what can be done and what cannot be done in the physical world, rule their capabilities in the spirit world."

"How are they hindered?" I asked Olga. "I mean, in exactly what ways?"

"Well," she replied, "take for example, the whole business of transportation in the spirit world. To transport oneself there, one can walk leisurely to his destination or one can reach his goal in a flash by an impulse of his mind. Obviously the materialistic soul will cling to the solidity—as it comparatively appears to him—of the road, while the spiritualistic or more advanced soul will reach out mentally."

I nodded slowly, trying to swallow down this unique concept. Then I continued my questions. "I'm trying to keep some order about this—sort of a logical development in my thinking," I said. "So what is the next step after someone has died? What's up next?"

The departed one, Olga stated, will find in his new environment not only those people he loved on earth who had arrived in the spirit realm ahead of him, but even pets. The general effect that is achieved is one of normalcy and as close a duplica-

tion of the physical world as is possible under the circumstances. This is done to prevent the newcomer from becoming
alarmed and to ease him slowly into a painless adjustment.

Usually a departed soul finds himself dressed in his accus-
tomed clothes, such as would be worn on a visit to friends. This
is created mentally. Eventually this type of apparel is dis-
carded and replaced by the flowing robes with which people
are normally arrayed in the spirit world. However, the earth-
type garments can be donned again at a moment's notice
should the occasion arise when this is deemed necessary, as
when greeting a newly departed soul who would not understand or recognize the person in his spirit robes, or when
appearing to a clairvoyant to demonstrate continued existence after death.

In most cases, upon becoming an inhabitant of the spirit
world, one feels a need to rest. His need is purely a condition
of the mind that stems frequently from a preceding long illness, old age, or any kind of catastrophic, precipitating cause
of death. Rest, therefore, is not only encouraged but provided
for, as well. All the time that is wanted can be taken for this
because time as we know it does not exist in the spirit world
and has no importance unless activities are undertaken which
involve people on earth.

"Do people who are already established in the spirit world
need periods of rest?" I asked, as Olga paused in her description. "Do they sleep?"

"They do take periods of rest, when they choose," she replied, "but not because they get tired. They don't sleep regu-
larly, as we do—if that's what you mean."

"Do they live as we live?" I asked next. "Do they eat, drink,
bathe, et cetera?"

According to Olga, there is a tendency to follow the habits
of earth upon entry into the world of spirit because the mind
has been conditioned to the routine of eating, drinking, bath-

ing, sleeping, walking, and other normal activities, none of which is necessary in that other dimension. However, because it is a mental world, all activities that can be conceived in the mind can be indulged in. The new spirit soon learns to adapt to the new conditions. In the spiritual realm there is a cycle of operations which maintains perfection in every manifestation. There is no need for birth, death and decay—the processes associated with the physical attributes of man.

A new spirit is met and welcomed when he arrives just as he would be if he were making a visit to friends or relatives in a foreign city or country. He will be guided to his place of abode in which, by mental projection, he will find duplication of many of the things he treasured on earth. Here again, the purpose of these mental counterparts, which he stored in the spirit world by his thoughts, is to make him feel thoroughly "at home," to prevent any uneasiness or sensation of being alien.

"How does one occupy himself in the spirit world?" was my next query. "What does one do?"

Olga burst out laughing in reply. "Honey," she said, "you want me to draw up a diagram, don't you, with all the spaces filled in and labeled, like a map of the United States. Well, I'll tell you what I have been told and what I know from my psychic experiences."

In the spirit world, a person's native talents are quickly revealed. Circumstances on the earth may have kept a man in a position as a laborer, whereas, given the opportunity he could have proved himself as a philosopher. In the spirit world he would become a philosopher.

All branches of the arts and sciences are found in the spirit world. Each individual is allowed to follow the path of progress he desires. This always is in accordance with his native talents and in the field in which he will be most proficient. The economics of the spirit world do not permit square pegs to be put into round holes as so often occurs in earth life's waste.

Schools in the spirit world are referred to as halls of learning. There are no entrance examinations, and no tuition fees to pay. The only attendees are those who desire to teach and those who wish to learn. No one receives a salary for teaching. The periodic paycheck so important on earth is not needed in the spirit world, since there are no monthly payments to meet; and there are no taxes to pay. Progression is the reward, effort is the fee, everything is absolutely fair to everyone.

"You see," Olga interrupted her discourse, as from time to time she did," I've visited some of these halls of learning myself. One time—I remember it so well—when I was in the astral, I met my father and accompanied him to some lectures. How I wish I could repeat what the speakers said! I can only vividly recall sitting there, listening intently, and being completely enthralled."

Then she continued:

The opportunities for advancement in the spirit world are unlimited. There are no overcrowded classrooms; no teachers' strikes; no student riots; no integration problems; no cheating; the facilities are always adequate; perfect balance is maintained; the students advance strictly in accordance with their ability to learn. There is no pressure on the student; no deadlines to meet; no examinations, no tests. When the student is qualified he advances automatically because he is ready. The instructor is always available, the only requirements being the desire to learn on the part of the student, and the desire to teach on the part of the instructor.

Meditation is practiced in the spirit world as on earth. Those who meditate in silence, in harmony, and in love, on their highest conception of the Supreme Being, find themselves coming into closer and closer touch with higher and higher spiritual forces. This brings about a refinement of the spiritual body and permits the spirit to advance to a brighter environment in which it will have further opportunities for progress.

Now it was my turn to interrupt Olga. "I don't quite understand that last point you made. What do you mean by a spirit's 'advance to a brighter environment'? You've consistently spoken of the 'spirit world' thus far. How can there be different environments?"

"'In my Father's house are many mansions,'" quoted Olga. "Personally, I've never been able to figure out where the churches got heaven and hell from—unless it was some hangover from the old pagan religions. Certainly Jesus made it plain enough! Actually there are many different levels of existence in the spirit world and each level represents a measure or stage of spiritual understanding or development of the souls who dwell there. People of like nature band together and stay together. They do so because they cannot bear it or even endure for long if they reach out of their normal spiritual level —although they are at liberty to do so."

Olga elaborated on this whole theme in much depth. There are no fences, she declared, or boundary walls in the spirit world to keep the inhabitants of the different levels apart. Nevertheless, the fact is that you cannot move far from the spiritual level you have attained without feeling uncomfortable. It is possible with training to travel into lower spiritual regions for the purpose of helping those who wish to better their environment. The sensation felt is similar to that experienced on earth when you travel from a warm dry region to a cold damp region. The spiritual light is dimmer and there is a grayish mist pervading the landscape. The spiritual vegetation is coarser in appearance and less luxuriant. After such a mission it is necessary to return to the natural level for rest and recharging.

Apart, however, from these occasional visits by those from more advanced spiritual levels to instruct those on the lower levels who are genuinely seeking higher knowledge, attempts to move into higher realms before adapting oneself by spiritual improvement will meet with failure. The sensation experienced in trying to transport the spiritual body across the higher frontier of the normal level is like going into the rarefied area at great altitudes; a sleepiness takes over and consciousness is lost. Upon the return of consciousness the familiar surroundings of the normal level come into view.

By the same token, an individual's actual spiritual state of being can never be concealed or misrepresented. It is expressed in the spirit world by the environment in which a person exists. Thus, while the home to which he is led will be similar to the one inhabited on earth, it will also reflect the true character of his thinking. A person whose thoughts are dark, with many things to hide, will find his spirit home in keeping with his thinking, containing plenty of dark corners in which to keep his secrets. The person who lived a life of true service to mankind, though in humble circumstances on earth, will find his home in the spirit world a place of beauty, enhanced by the loving thoughts of those he served on earth, and by the deep appreciation of the ones he aided in the spirit world.

Even the clothing worn in the spirit world reveals plainly and conspicuously the spiritual state of the wearer. Spirit robes, by way of illustration, like environment are in strict keeping with the character of the spirit being. At any particular level of spiritual existence, the robes of all residents are similar in radiance, since it is the brightness of the garments which depicts the degree of spirituality, and this degree of spirituality, in turn, is approximately the same at any one level of spiritual existence. In this way, visitors from higher levels can be recognized immediately by the unusual brightness of their attire which is conspicuously different from that worn by the regular inhabitants. In fact, if the level of a visitor is much higher than the level to which he has descended, he will mentally have to subdue the brightness of his appearance before he can be observed by those he has come to teach.

"In other words," Olga concluded this portion of her speech, "truth is dominant in the spiritual world. It cannot be distorted as it is in the physical world through language limitations, deliberate concealment, and all the other ruses which are used to make it hard to perceive. It is absolutely impossible to pass oneself for something one is not; one cannot appear as a saint or a seer if the level of his thought does not match his protestations."

I was silent briefly while I attempted to assimilate this. It was not that simple to formulate a considered opinion after all that I had just heard, but one thing seemed somewhat unclear to me.

"Olga," I said, "how much of this hereafter that you describe conforms to orthodox Christian thology? Is it consistent with it?"

"Is orthodox Christian theology consistent?" she countered. "There are many different conceptions of what exactly takes place after death. There are those who believe that the physical body lies in the grave until a trumpet sounds, and when this is heard the dead all rise from their graves. If this is to be, we should have a population explosion like none that has previously occurred, or even been anticipated. There are others who believe the soul is transported after death to one of two places. One is reserved for the believers in their particular religion, and called by various names, one of which is 'heaven'; the other is reserved for all others, and is called by various other names, one of which is 'hell.' Between these two extremes there are many other beliefs."

"Agreed," I responded.

"Well," she went on, "I would say that everything that I have seen of the spirit world is consistent with the Christianity of Jesus. Take the dominance of truth, for example. Is that unchristian? Take, also, the principle of accountability.

Granted that there is no heaven or hell as such. Still, grada-
tions of both exist. We pass over to the next world in exactly
the same mental state of spiritual development which we had
when we left this world, and we are accommodated there on
the basis of that development or lack of development. Worthy
ones will have a place prepared for them commensurate with
their service to God and to their fellow men. This is unmutable
law. It is true, also, that dark conditions exist in the spirit
world. There dwell the unenlightened ones, the sponsors of
hate and greed. They are from all levels of society on earth,
but are on the same level in the spirit world because they
share the same level of spiritual development. If one wishes to
avoid a period in the lower levels, one must live a life of
unselfish service, as expressed in that great commandment:
'Love one another.'

"Is that unchristian?" she challenged.

"Of course not!" There was no question about this left in my
mind.

"All right." She sounded more mollified. "Now consider this:
certainly, our thoughts and actions here create the environment in which we will live there. But, from what I have been
shown of the spirit world, I know as a fact that sooner or later
almost every soul feels a stirring within his consciousness that
urges him onward to seek a higher level. When he follows that
urge, he is always encouraged and helped by teachers from
the higher, brighter levels along the path of spiritual progress."

She paused for a sip of water, and then continued. "There
are many ways to die and many ways to be received into the
spirit world. Some die young of natural causes, others live to
a ripe old age before leaving the body. Many go as a result of
accidents or war or suicide or through some other destructive
force. No matter what the cause of death may be—no matter

what!—the spirit lives on. No soul is ever lost, and the pathway to brighter and better conditions is always open. That is God's decree."

Olga made this summation almost triumphantly and I looked at her somewhat wistfully. "It's beautiful," I said, completely sincere. "Everything you've described depicts the kind of perfect, equitable, and beautiful afterlife that anyone could dream of."

"But it's a lot to swallow." She didn't ask me. She told me. Then she smiled. "Honey, I understand exactly how you feel. Not that I ever had your kind of doubt. I have always trusted my psychic experiences and they give me quite an edge on the ordinary believer. Besides that, though, I have had further proof recently that has ended even any subconscious unbelief I may have unknowingly had. Shall we go into that tomorrow?"

"Tomorrow?" I echoed indignantly. "Why not now?"

"Tomorrow," she repeated firmly. "We've had a long day of it already."

"Okay, tomorrow it is," I agreed reluctantly, gathering up my purse, briefcase, and car keys in order to go.

As I started down the front path of Olga's house, I turned once more to wave goodbye. She was standing in the doorway, with the lamplight from the living room behind her creating a kind of radiance around her head and with the brightness of her wholehearted smile lighting up her face.

I stopped for a moment, just to look, and how I envied her that calm assurance, that unreserved conviction! As she was, so must the early Christians have been in the face of their detractors: full of faith and spiritual peace. As I was, comparatively, so must Paul have been before he started on the road to Damascus.

Slowly I turned away, wondering deep down inside me if

tomorrow's session would make me better able to share Olga
Worrall's vision; if somehow, at last, I would begin to see,
figuratively, even just a little bit of what she saw so completely,
so inspirationally, and so literally!

CHAPTER VII

Telephone between Two Worlds

THE following morning I arrived at Olga Worrall's house eagerly, expectantly, but more uncertain of what might be forthcoming next than the first astronaut must have been when he took off on his first trip to the moon. In fact, the more I thought about it, the more perplexed I became. What further proof of Olga's psychically discerned hereafter could there be unless—and I nearly ran straight through a red light as the idea suddenly hit me—it was the testimony of someone who had died and come back!

Obviously, such an absurd notion was shrugged off mentally almost as soon as it was born. Nevertheless, it was partial conditioning, at least, for the denouement which followed: the testimony of someone who had died and *reported* back.

Olga began almost immediately after I entered. She was seated at the dining-room table, still over her breakfast tea and toast, when she said: "Honey, do you remember when Ambrose made the change?"

"Made the change," I knew from having heard the expression before, was Olga's way of saying "died." Ambrose, as I was well aware, had passed on unexpectedly on February 2, 1972, almost midway in the course of my visits to research Olga. It had been a tragic happening—not only as such an event ordinarily is, but even more so because of the long, close relationship between this husband and wife. They had been married for forty-four years; they had worked together throughout that time, they had shared the same interests and been dedicated to the same spiritual goals; they had lived together in a kind of warmth and love and harmony that was as visible and identifiable to those around them as the hair on their heads.

I don't think I will ever forget the beauty of the memorial service for Ambrose Worrall which I attended a few days after he went and which was held in the Mount Washington Methodist Church in Baltimore—the same church where Olga holds her regular New Life Clinic. Instead of death, there was an affirmation of life; instead of despair, there was a feeling of purposefulness. The church was overfilled; the simple casket was tightly sealed; the hymns that were sung were vibrant declarations of faith and hope, especially the swelling rendition of Ambrose's favorite "How Great Thou Art"; the brief messages that were given by the minister and the bishop were low-keyed, sincere, temporary farewells to a good and treasured friend.

Olga came in by herself, red-eyed and sad-faced, but very straight and tall. She was dressed beautifully and elegantly, her bearing no less dignified or proud than a British queen on her way to the cathedral. As she moved down the aisle to a front pew, she paused again and again to nod silently at someone whom she apparently recognized, or else to murmer a soft "Hello." It was an admirable and memorable performance.

Recalling all of this in a flash as Olga asked her question, I immediately answered, "Of course I remember when Ambrose made the change. Why?"

Instead of answering my question, Olga asked me another. "And do you remember how absolutely beside myself I was?" she went on, apparently intent on pursuing her own line of thought.

"Yes." I remembered that very well, too.

Olga had asked me to be at her house the day after the memorial service to see if I could help her sort out Ambrose's records and papers. "I want to get things in some decent kind of order," she told me over the telephone. "Will you come?"

I came. Actually, I was glad to be able to be of any assistance. It was a revelation, moreover, to see Olga in a more private role than that displayed the day before.

"Naturally I've been crying," she replied when I commented on her swollen eyes as I came in. "Why shouldn't I cry?" she demanded belligerantly. "I can't bear it when people expect me never to grieve because I, of all people, know that Ambrose isn't really dead and that I'll see him again. So what? Sure, I don't despair and I know beyond all doubt that we'll be together again! But can't they understand that I'm alone *now?* Can't they realize that he's there and I'm here— and I'm here alone, all by myself, and that it's almost more than I can bear?"

The tears streamed down her face as she wept like a little child who has just lost his only, most precious possession. Suddenly she was no longer a woman with years of mature living behind her. She *was* just a child—the child that hides eternally inside all of us and never grows up; the child who will not listen to reason or experience but howls for what he wants when there is no way to get it, who stands in the middle of nowhere and demands an ice-cream cone right now!

There was nothing I could do, however, except murmur my sympathy and set about plowing through Ambrose's papers— which I did with Olga's help. She stopped crying, of course, and did help, but it was pitifully plain to see that the icy hand of loneliness had already gripped its cold fingers tightly about her heart. She was even able—and nothing speaks more eloquently of her degree of emotional shock than the fact that she doesn't remember this incident at all to this very day!—to

psychically find some stock certificates I had apparently mis-
laid by going into another room, by sitting quietly there by
herself to ask for spiritual help, and by then returning to produce the missing papers immediately from a pile I had vainly
searched just minutes before.

"What are you getting at, Olga?" I prodded her tactfully,
feeling myself disturbed once more at the memory of her deep
sorrow. "It was a terrible time for you. I know that."

Again she ignored my question and asked another of her
own. "And did you ever stop to realize how soon I was able to
regain my self-control and resume an even increased schedule
of activities? And did you ever wonder how or why?"

With a momentary sense of surprise, I said promptly: "The
answer to both of those is No."

As I thought about it, though, in response to Olga's mention
of it just then, I was definitely conscious of the fact that what
she had said was indeed so; that she had made a remarkable
and rapid recovery from any show of bereavement. Not, as I
thought about it further, that my previous unawareness of this
accomplishment was at all startling. Grief, at best, makes us
somewhat uncomfortable if only because there is usually nothing that we can do to help the one who is grieving. It speaks
of a kind of psychological nakedness that makes us either turn
away in embarrassment or wait awkwardly for the passage of
time to cover it up with the appearance of outward normalcy.
This last, apparently, was what I had done—glad, only, that
Olga soon seemed herself again.

"Of course you just took it for granted," Olga commented
before I could say a word. "People always do," she added drily.
Then she continued, "But that's not the point I'm trying to
make. What I am trying to tell you is that I could emerge from
that deep-down blackness as quickly as I did because Ambrose
helped me."

"*Ambrose* helped you?" I echoed blankly. "How could Ambrose help you—Oh, you know what I mean—he was gone!"

Olga smiled. "Gone?" She repeated. "Only in a physical sense, Edwina. Actually, he began contacting me almost from the very day he made the change." She paused briefly, then stood up and said, "Come on in the library, honey, and I'll get out the records I've kept about my communications with Ambrose. Just let me put these few dishes in the sink."

"Did you say 'communications'?" I asked, standing up also and following Olga into the kitchen. "How many are there and how do you get them?"

Olga burst out laughing as she headed next for the library. "If you don't make it sound like some kind of a telephone hook-up!" she declared. "Listen, child, it's not that simple yet —although there are some psychic investigators who honestly believe that the day will come when spirit voices will be audible through some kind of machine that will lower spirit vibrations to our level. Then we can talk back and forth by going into the contraption—just about the same way we go into a telephone booth now, put in the appropriate coins, and get Europe."

We were in the library now and Olga brought over a big looseleaf notebook and a pile of papers to where I had parked myself on the couch. "These," she said, her voice and face taking on a tone of absolute seriousness, "are my communications. As for the 'how,' let me try to explain. Originally I saw Ambrose a few times with my physical eyes and heard his voice—telepathically or physically. I don't really know. Then, when I would sit in the nine o'clock silent-time for absent prayer, I became aware that Ambrose was there too. Gradually I could hear his voice—not aloud—but as if in my head and there were whole messages, almost letters, you might say, that came through. Since I could never remember them all, however much I wanted to, I began to write his words down. Now, at any time of the day or night, when I go into the silence, we communicate. I send him unspoken thoughts and I write down his reply."

Olga made this amazing statement as matter-of-factly as a newscaster reads off the daily baseball scores. In response, and while I was still reeling mentally from the effects of trying to visualize the entire procedure, I asked, in a deliberately similar, mundane tone of voice, "And are you implying that Ambrose's messages to you have confirmed what you have already told me about the hereafter?"

"I am not implying anything," Olga corrected me, "I am *telling* you. They have not merely confirmed many things, but they have clarified and amplified as well." She paused at this point and laughed. "Honey," she told me in her usual, discerning way, "stop trying to talk about all this as if we were discussing the merits of the delicatessen section of the local supermarket. I realize how this must shock you. It's spectacular! But it's true; and maybe if you listen to how it all began and developed, you will understand it better."

Olga said that she had never thought consciously, at first, of establishing any direct communication with Ambrose. In the very evening, however, of the day on which he died, he appeared to her. She had stretched out on their bed in a state of total desolation and exhaustion, too numb, almost, to think of anything at all, when suddenly she saw Ambrose clearly and unequivocally standing beside the bed.

"He clasped my hands in his," she said, "in his own very special way—just as he always used to do. Then he told me," and she turned quickly to read from a sheet of paper, "'I'm allright, sweetheart; all is well with me. Our sons and our friends over here gave me a royal welcome. Don't cry, dear, don't cry.'"

There were tears of joy in Olga's eyes as she put the paper down.

"You both saw and heard him?" I asked, before she could continue.

"Definitely," she replied. "Actually, I've *seen* Ambrose only a few times. Mostly, I just *hear* him—and sometimes I don't even hear him, either. I just feel his words impressed upon my mind telepathically. For example: a few days after this incident, on the morning of the memorial service, he spoke to me as I lay in bed, reluctant to get up and dreading the public appearance I knew I had to make. He said—not that I saw him, mind you, only that I heard him distinctly—" and here again, Olga referred to some written notes: "'Today, sweetheart, we will return to Mother Nature my physical body that served me so well. I am surrounded here by our team of helpers, as well as friends and relatives.'"

"What 'team of helpers'?" I asked, puzzled.

"Our spirit helpers," Olga replied. "The spirit entities with whom we have been involved in our psychic work all through the years. Those who have helped us right along."

While she was explaining, Olga was leafing through some of the other papers in her hand. Abruptly she stopped and pulled out a page on which, in longhand, there was a date at the top and a paragraph of writing. "Oh, here's one experience I remember so well," she exclaimed excitedly. "This was one of the few instances when Ambrose was both visible as well as audible to me. It happened in those same early weeks after he passed on. I was right here in the library, at the table there, trying to straighten up the papers he had left spread out just the day before he left his body behind. I burst into tears suddenly, and all at once, in that very moment, Ambrose appeared, materialized briefly at my side. His face was so very sad and he just stood and stared at me so hard and long—though it must have been only a few seconds! I knew he was upset because I was weeping and I heard him tell me not to cry. Then he disappeared—completely vanished from my physical sight."

Olga sighed as she finished this account. "He was so close, so near to me, so distinct!" she said, looking across at me with a wistful smile. "I could almost have held him in my arms."

I looked back at her sympathetically. "It must have been a moving experience," I agreed, "even if it might only have been something you imagined—sort of like a dream."

"A dream!" Olga groaned. "Honey, you still don't understand. I was awake and it was real! Besides, Ambrose has come through to Harold Sherman, too, and—"

"Who is Harold Sherman?" I interrupted.

"Good Lord!" Olga groaned again. "I keep forgetting what a novice you are in this whole field. Well, for your information, Harold Sherman is a legendary researcher and practitioner in the field of spiritual healing. He heads the ESP Research Associates Foundation and took part, incidentally, in some amazing, successful experiments in telepathy with Sir Hubert Wilkins when Sir Hubert was off on one of his North Pole expeditions many years ago. Harold also runs an annual Body, Mind and Spirit Healing Workshop; he writes extensively; and as important as anything else, he is an old, old friend." Olga rounded off this list of Mr. Sherman's credentials with a big sigh. Then she promptly resumed her original point. "When Ambrose made the change," she said, "I called Harold to tell him what had happened. Within a few hours, Harold called me back to say that he and his wife, Martha, had gone into the silence and that he was impressed mentally with a message from Ambrose: 'Tell Olga—oh, what a beautiful morning!'"

Olga stopped speaking at this point, obviously savoring those few words again, and I found myself impulsively paraphrasing them. "Oh, what a beautiful message," I exclaimed, "especially from someone who has just died!"

Olga nodded. "But that's not all," she continued. On the fourth of February, 1972, just two days after Ambrose's passing, Harold received another message from Ambrose. It was apparently in the astral and Harold wrote it down as soon as he regained full consciousness." She paused once more to search through her batch of written materials. "Oh, here it is," she said, handing me an envelope with two typewritten sheets inside. "Harold sent it to me as soon as he recorded it. See the date? February the fourth, 1972. And see the letterhead: from Arkansas, where Harold lives."

I took the two pages and sat back to read Harold Sherman's transcription of what Ambrose Worrall had told him. There was no heading on the paper and no salutation; it was, in form, more of a memorandum, and it simply stated:

"Tell Olga I am so happy that she had kept my body at home which I now look upon as the instrument that gave me such faithful service all my wonderful earth years with her. Tell her XYZ had things in charge during my transition and I was almost immediately conscious in what we call the spirit body. I have no way of telling you how wonderful it is . . . there is nothing truer than the immortality of the soul. . . .

"Tell Olga she must rest for a few months so we can help restore her physical vitality and renew her spirit. Tell her she will be guided in her choice of places and organizations to serve, and that I will always be with her . . . but she is not to wear herself out by taking on many engagements and she is to keep the nine o'clock hour which means so much to many.

"Olga's work at the New Life Clinic should continue because I am eager to conduct new healing experiments through her, which I can only do from this side of life. Olga will soon get evidence of these additional healing powers and she will be prepared for one of the finest healing demonstrations of her life when you work with her at the Healing Workshop in Hot Springs. It is a fact that some healers have former doctors and surgeons working through them and I will be shown the way by XYZ and others how to work through Olga. When she lays her hands on those seeking healings, my hands will be there with hers.

"In time, I will be able to carry on my own studies of these healing energies and reveal them through Olga, who can demonstrate them. It is always a shock to leave so suddenly. Had I not been prepared through our way of life and had Olga not released me—despite her own shock and grief—it would have been difficult.

"You wonder, Harold, if I really did appear to you in your mind, when you and Martha were meditating on me after receiving the news of my passing—and whether I really *did* say to you mentally, 'Tell Olga—Oh, what a beautiful morning!' Those were my exact words—and it *is* a beautiful morning to all who are prepared to make the transition and who awaken on this side of life. It is always morning here. The 'sun of the spirit' is always rising. Olga's finest work is still ahead of her. And, best of all, we will still be working together.

"You are to write this down, Harold, as soon as you become conscious in your physical body—because you have been in a higher state with me, which you will always regard as a dream —and which you may even have difficulty in believing."

The message ended thus abruptly, with no customary closing and with no added comment from Harold Sherman. When I finished reading it, I told Olga earnestly: "What a great joy it must have been to receive this letter! What a comfort such a communication must be!"

"It was a joy to receive Harold's message," she agreed, "and it is a comfort to hear, in any way, from my darling. But my communications with Ambrose mean a lot more than that. They mean much, much more to me!"

"What more do they mean?" I asked.

"Well, to begin with," Olga answered, "I get advice and guidance from Ambrose whenever I need any." She stopped suddenly and started to laugh. "Why, even this book project we've embarked upon has received his wholehearted blessing, Edwina. When I asked him in the silence if I should continue along with it with you, he said"—and she searched in the looseleaf notebook until she found the pertinent page—'Edwina has a great deal to learn about the psychic world but she will do a good job with the material you can give her. She is sincere and writes beautifully. XYZ and some of the others here will help her, too. We are excited about the book.'"

I stared in amazement at the page with these words on it—dated several months back. Then I asked Olga, remembering that the designation had appeared also in Harold Sherman's message: "Who or what is XYZ?"

"That's our reference to a particular spirit entity who has worked with Ambrose and me for years," Olga explained. "He is actually a highly evolved spirit who chooses not to have his name used."

"Oh." What else was there for me to say? Besides, I suddenly realized that I must have been becoming somewhat more inured to the whole concept of spirit entities, anyway, since for the first time, more or less, since the initiation of my research, I didn't find myself squirming about to avoid stepping on invisible toes! Instead I said to Olga, as matter-of-factly as if she had merely passed along a favorable comment from a mutual friend who had just been visiting, "Well, I'm glad Ambrose and XYZ approve of me."

She laughed in reply. "That was just a for-instance," she said merrily. Then, growing more serious, she elaborated on her original theme. "When I say my communications with Ambrose mean a lot more to me than just the usual type of greeting-card reassurances most people associate with mediumistic messages, I am referring to a kind of spiritual correspondence that is pertinent and almost businesslike in its scope. Also, it's definitely clairvoyant and looks ahead into the future."

I tried to translate this reply into specifics I could understand. "Are you saying," I asked slowly, "that Ambrose tells you what is going to happen next?"

"Tells me, forewarns me, and sometimes advises me where

decisions have to be made," Olga replied. "Perhaps a few concrete illustrations would enable you to see how he and I have become a new kind of working team—if a most unorthodox one. Let me see," she murmured thoughtfully, glancing down again at the papers she had just put aside. "Oh yes, let's go back to this Sherman letter as a start. See here where Harold said that Ambrose said that my healing powers would be enhanced, that he would work through me, that I should continue the New Life Clinic, and that my participation in the Hot Springs Healing Workshop would produce 'one of the finest healing demonstrations' of my life? See it?"

"Yes," I answered expectantly.

"Well," she said, giving me some pages from the notebook to read, "I was getting very similar messages from Ambrose myself. You know, we had always done things together as much as possible. I had never even traveled without him before—so that when he passed on, I hesitated about going to conferences alone. Day after day, though, he kept urging me to take up our work where he had left off. He kept impressing me, whenever I sat in the silence, that my powers would be enhanced, that his hands would be working through my hands. When the Hot Springs Healing Workshop was coming up, I told Harold Sherman that I wasn't sure I would go. That night, though"—and she pulled out a page to show me—"Ambrose came through and not only insisted that I go, but assured me, as he had Harold before, that it would prove to be 'one of the finest healing demonstrations' of my life."

She paused here and I inserted quickly, "So you went?"

"So I went," she affirmed, "and it was one of the finest healing demonstrations of my life."

"What happened?" I asked.

"Oh, there were many healings," she replied enthusiastically. "One woman had a lump disappear from her breast; there were healings of back pain—and many others. But one healing occurred which I will never, never forget! It still thrills me!"

Apparently, during the course of the Healing Workshop, an elderly couple arrived late one night at the hotel where the workshop was being held. They had no idea that there was such a workshop in existence, much less that it was taking place. They had, unfortunately, got lost on their way home to Chicago and had simply decided to stay overnight at this particular hotel because it was getting too dark to push on anymore that day.

With the couple was their granddaughter—in a wheelchair. She was about twenty years old and, according to their testimony, completely retarded: she had never talked or walked in her life. In the morning, after a night's rest, they decided to go into the hotel dining-room for breakfast before resuming their journey. It was while they were going to eat, therefore, that they overheard a group on the hotel elevator talking about the Healing Workshop which they were obviously attending.

"What is this Healing Workshop about?" the grandmother asked the people in the nearby group when they were leaving the elevator.

"It's all about spiritual healing," was the reply. "Would you like to see some of the literature?"

One of the women produced a workshop brochure and stood by while the couple looked through it. She even gave one to the young girl in the wheelchair who turned the pages without any indication of interest at first until, suddenly, she began to point excitedly at the picture of Olga Worrall. The pathetically animalistic sounds and grunts that accompanied the gestures were totally incomprehensible, but the grandmother seemed to catch the meaning of what she was trying to say.

"Who is that lady?" she asked the woman who had let them

have the brochure. "I'd so like my granddaughter to get to see her."

"That's Olga Worrall," the woman replied. "She's a well-known spiritual healer. Why don't you come to our workshop this afternoon and Mrs. Worrall can do the laying-on of hands for her then?"

"We can't," the elderly gentleman replied firmly, speaking for himself and his wife. "We lost our way yesterday and we're behind schedule already." Then, in response to his wife's obvious, extreme regret, he asked: "Could Mrs. Worrall see us here? Now?"

A quick telephone call was made to Olga's room and, since Olga was about to come down for some breakfast herself, having just concluded an interview with the local press, she readily agreed to this impromptu arrangement.

When Olga arrived on the scene, the grandparents gave her a quick resume of their granddaughter's condition: her retardation since infancy, her inability to walk and talk. As Olga placed her hands on the girl, however, and stood looking down into the girl's eyes, she clairvoyantly was told that the girl was not retarded, but that she had become incapacitated after a bad fall when she was just a baby.

"Why, she did have a very bad fall out of her highchair when she was eight months old," exclaimed the grandmother excitedly. "She had seemed normal to us all up until then, but after that she never developed properly."

Olga finished the laying-on of hands, told the grandparents that she would pray for the girl, reminded them that healing comes from God—and turned away. "Remember," she repeated to them as they thanked her, "that there are no guarantees. I am only a channel. The power comes from God."

After Olga left, the woman who had given the couple the brochures stayed on a while to tell them some more about spiritual healing. Suddenly the girl in the wheelchair, who had

seemed surprisingly aware of, and responsive to, Olga's minis-
trations, began making some of those strange noises again.
Abruptly these stopped and, instead, clear sounds began to
emerge from between her struggling lips. To the amazement
of those around her—and a group had collected to watch Olga's healing treatment—she began to say one or two recognizable words.

"Dear God, she's speaking!" the grandfather said in hushed
tones, almost whispering, as if afraid to say it aloud.

"Say 'Grandma,'" the woman with the brochures told the
girl, also trying to remain calm.

"Grammer," repeated the girl slowly.

Almost immediately, pandemonium broke out. The grandmother began to sob hysterically; the people standing by
broke into excited exclamations; the people who were farther
off came rushing over to find out what was going on.

"It was sort of like a miracle," Olga remembered with won-
derment in her voice. "I had already left the room when it
happened, but I heard all about it many times over from some
of those who witnessed it. Just hearing about it, though, as I did
after the people drove off, was thrilling enough."

"It was a miracle," I agreed. "Did you ever get any follow-
up?"

"I had one report from Chicago a few months afterward,"
Olga said. "Her talking was improving and she was beginning
to walk. The whole thing was exactly as Ambrose had promised: 'one of the finest healing demonstrations' of my entire life
—and the seemingly coincidental way in which it came about
convinces me of that more than ever. There is no such thing
as true coincidence. The whole concept of coincidence is but
narrow, human rationalization for God's deliberate invention
and intervention. That healing was not really any accidental
happening."

She was obviously almost as impressed with the fulfillment

of Ambrose's promise in the entire event as with the healing itself. Realizing this, I asked, "Do Ambrose's predictions for you usually come true?"

"Usually," Olga replied. "His forewarnings about future happenings are generally correct. Sometimes he changes his own forecasts, of course, but that's because, while he can see further ahead from the other side than we can see, he still can't see completely ahead. But," she added even more emphatically, "when he makes a promise to me, he always keeps it."

Once again Olga rummaged through her stack of papers and I could see she was looking for something special. I waited with growing curiosity, therefore, until she finally exclaimed, "Oh, here it is!" and gave me a thick envelope.

"Before you read this," she said, "let me explain a few things by way of preliminary. About a year ago, if you remember, I spent some six weeks lecturing and healing in Japan. When the invitation came, I was afraid to undertake such a long journey alone. Ambrose, however, insisted that I go and assured me all would be well and a great deal would be accomplished. Finally, since I was being very difficult to convince, he gave me this promise—" and here she read aloud from her looseleaf book: "'I will go to Japan with you. You shall see the evidence of it there.'"

She paused for a while, reminiscently, and I could contain myself no longer. "Did you?" I asked impatiently.

It took Olga a few moments before she was ready to reply. "He appeared to one of the Japanese professors," she finally said. "The man was so positive that Ambrose was beside me on the platform that he invited *both* of us to his house. He was a man, incidentally, who had never had a psychic experience before in his entire life, and he was most amazed. He described Ambrose perfectly to me—although he had never even seen a picture of Ambrose—and just recently, on a visit to Baltimore, he came to my home and identified a photo of Ambrose as a photo of the man he had seen with me in Japan. Can you imagine anything more evidential? If I had seen Ambrose, it would be open to all the usual charges of imagination, wishful thinking, et cetera, such as you implied before. But the fact that Ambrose was visualized by someone else—someone who had never seen Ambrose when Ambrose was alive and someone who saw Ambrose without my even knowing it had happened until he stood up in a church service and told about it afterward—all of this makes it a most significant occurrence."

"It certainly does," I agreed wholeheartedly. "By the way, Olga, who is this 'someone' who saw Ambrose?"

She burst out laughing. "Checking again, Edwina? Okay, let me assure you he is no kook, no illiterate, no easily persuaded individual. He is what lawyers would call an authoritative or expert witness. His name is Dr. Adachi; he holds a doctorate in political science and is a professor of law at Kwansei Gakuin University in Japan since 1946; he is fifty-seven years old; he is a Christian and—" Suddenly, Olga interrupted herself. "Why am I telling you all this? I asked Dr. Adachi to tell his entire experience in his own words and send it to me. That letter in your own hand is his complete and unexpurgated account—he even talks about my big nose!" She laughed again. "Go on, Edwina, read it. It's fascinating and I just love the Japanese way in which he describes everything and the official-looking signature at the end. It has the sound of someone testifying under oath—and I think he meant it that way. You know, he is a lawyer."

Even while Olga was still speaking, I opened the thick envelope postmarked Japan. Then I took out the several sheets of paper that were neatly folded inside and read the following:

"Before I speak about the mysterious experience I had about Mr. Worrall, I would like to introduce myself briefly.

"I was born in 1917. I graduated from Kyoto University and have been a professor at the Law Department, Kwansei Gakuin University, since 1946. My major is political science, especially the field of public administration. Since 1971 I have been in the position of the President of the Japanese Society for Public Administration. I have been considering myself as an egocentric positivist. I regard myself more like Thomas than Thomas himself who said, 'Except I shall see in his hands the print of the nails, and put my finger into the print of the nails, and put my hand into his side, I will not believe' (John 20:25). The other day, for instance, before telling them about the mysterious experience, I said to five colleagues of mine, political scientists, 'Do you think that I am more like Thomas than Thomas himself?' And instantly all of them said, 'Yes.' One of them even said, 'You give me a hard time, examining my dissertations strictly, because you are such a positivist as Thomas.'

"It was in November, 1972, that I first learned the name of Mrs. Worrall, a celebrated American spiritual healer, and her coming to Japan, from Dr. Bray, a very good friend of mine and a professor at the Theological Department of Kwansei Gakuin University. Since I understood that she was coming to Japan by herself, I supposed she was a widow.

"Mrs. Worrall came to Japan in March, 1973, and visited Shukugawa-Higashi Church, our church, on Sunday, April 1. This little church was established in 1961 mainly through the effort of Dr. Bray. My wife and I attended the service, but since we arrived a few minutes late, we sat on the rear seat. There were about fifty attendants at most. Mrs. Worrall was already on the platform about ten inches higher than the floor. And clearly did I see Mr. Worrall sitting beside her. Vividly do I remember that I was looking at him considering Mrs. Worrall was not a widow after all. If I am allowed to speak frankly about something which might sound impolite to Mrs. Worrall,

she was sitting with her hat and shoes on, which isn't a good
manner from a Japanese point of view. I well understand the
difference between the American manners and the Japanese
ones. But at any rate, such a manner of hers and her big nose
impressed her haughtiness on my mind. Therefore, compar-
ing her with my obedient wife sitting by my side, I sympa-
thized with Mr. Worrall who was married to this arrogant-
looking lady with mysterious power by a psychology peculiar
to Japanese men while looking at him. Let me add that since
we yellow Japanese and white Americans apparently look different, anyone present there can assure you that except for
Mr. & Mrs. Worrall and Mr. & Mrs. Bray, all the attendants of
the day were Japanese.

"On that day Mrs. Worrall spoke about her spiritual healing.
After the service was over, Mrs. Worrall was introduced to
each attendant at the rear door. She was, of course, introduced
to me and my wife also. Right after that I said to my wife, 'Why
isn't Mr. Worrall introduced?' She replied, 'What nonsense are
you talking about?' On that day we did not discuss it any
further as the exit was crowded and it was quite noisy there.

"The Brays and our family have been associating in quite a
friendly way. Dr. and Mrs. Bray attended the wedding ceremony of Kuriko, our oldest daughter, representing Kwansei
Gakuin University and Shukugawa-Higashi Church, while my
wife and I joined that of Tommy, the Brays' second oldest son,
at Winnipeg, Canada, representing the university and the
church. It was natural, therefore, that I wanted to invite the
Worralls, the Brays' guests, to our house. After talking about
it with Dr. Bray, I bade my wife, who does not speak English,
'I am going to invite the four Americans to our house on April
18. Prepare sukiyaki for them and us.' Although I give lectures
on democratic government and democratic administration at
college, I am the Emperor at home, a generous one, however.
My wife who is my faithful subject made no objection to it and

obeyed me. Later she said that she felt something strange about my bidding. Anyway it was a fact that I told my wife to prepare a meal for four American guests. This can be witnessed by my wife and daughter.

"At five o'clock in the afternoon, on April 18, our guests appeared at the front of my house. But I couldn't find Mr. Worrall among them. Mrs. Worrall and the Brays were all that came. So I said to them, 'Why didn't Mr. Worrall come?' The three guests can witness the fact that I gave them this question. Then Dr. Bray said, 'Mr. Worrall died last year.' I was terribly sorry that I had said such an impolite thing to Mrs. Worrall. I tried to apologize to her. But my mind was too confused to say anything further.

"The sukiyaki party was a pleasant one. But since we were going to attend a prayer meeting at the church in the evening, where Mrs. Worrall was going to give a healing service, we had to end the party in about two hours. After my wife and I came home from the service, I talked with my wife. I said to her, 'Didn't you see Mr. Worrall at the April 1 service?' And her reply was absolutely in the negative. I again said to her, 'Didn't you see a male Caucasian besides Dr. Bray?' Again she said, 'No.' Whenever there was a difference in opinion between us couple, I used to force mine upon her. I can certainly assure you of the following: if I had not heard about Mr. Worrall's death from Dr. Bray that evening, I would have claimed to my wife, 'You are wrong. You were simply too careless to notice Mr. Worrall's presence.' But in this case it was a fact that I was wrong. In the diary of the night I wrote, 'I believed I saw Mr. Worrall, but he was already dead. How strange!' From then on, however, I tried to forget that I saw Mr. Worrall as best I could. Even when I recalled it now and then, I tried to persuade myself, saying, 'You simply saw a vision,' and efface the memory from my mind.

"On Sunday May 6, I went to church earlier than usual so

as to give a talk at the Sunday School service. I don't remember what I spoke about there. Nor does my diary of the day mention it. Considering this, it seems that I was fairly successful in forgetting that I had seen Mr. Worrall. On that day our Japanese minister was supposed to give a sermon for the adults' service, but the program was changed and Mrs. Worrall gave a 'Questions and Answers' program. The same kind of programs she had held in some other churches of Japan accorded a favorable reception, and besides, since she was going home the next day, she wanted to say goodbye to our church. Mrs. Worrall appeared about ten-twenty-five with Dr. and Mrs. Bray. All of a sudden I vividly recalled Mr. Worrall. The entrance to the chapel was crowded. Mrs. Bray was not talking with anyone, and so I talked to her. 'Have you ever seen Mr. Worrall? I really saw him on April 1. That's why I asked how come Mr. Worrall was not with you when you came to my house the other day. He is not a tall man and—' Then Mrs. Bray said, 'I have never met Mr. Worrall. I have only seen the picture of his upper half. So I can't tell how tall he is.' As the service was about to start, I stopped talking and went into the chapel.

"The service went on as usual and Mrs. Worrall stood where the minister usually stands and made a brief speech and asked the congregation to give her any questions about spiritual healing.

"It took me a great deal of courage but I started to speak to Mrs. Worrall and the congregation about my experience concerning Mr. Worrall in Japanese. I said, 'I am going to speak about what you may not be able to believe at all. But many people can witness that it is a fact.' Mr. Ohinata, a young member of the church, interpreted to Mrs. Worrall for me. I continued, 'I did see Mr. Worrall. He was not a tall man but had a round face. He was a little fat and had glasses with a black frame on.' When these words were translated to Mrs.

Worrall, she said, 'What Prof. Adachi has just mentioned was the real characteristics my husband used to own.' The questions and answers between me and Mrs. Worrall through the interpreter lasted about fifteen minutes. What she said then can be more accurately told by Mrs. Worrall herself. But I do remember this one thing Mrs. Worrall said: "My husband told me before my departure for Japan that he would accompany me to Japan.' After the service I shook hands with her and said, 'I still remember Mr. Worrall. He was in a blue and grey suit.' 'My husband used to wear a blue and grey suit all the time,' Mrs. Worrall said and dropped some tears.

"I have told this strange experience to my family and friends. But since I knew that while talking about his experience many times, one tends to review and improve it so that it may suit himself, I made some memoranda to record the event accurately upon which I am writing this.

"On August 16, 1973, my wife and I together with our two daughters and the husband of the older daughter made a tour of Europe and came home on September 3. Soon after that my wife and I left Japan for Canada to attend the wedding ceremony of Tommy, the second oldest son of the Brays, held in the suburbs of Winnipeg. And from there we went down to the United States and on September 24 we were in Washington, D.C. After finishing my work there, I called up Mrs. Worrall in Baltimore. The following afternoon, on September 27, we saw Mrs. Worrall and a few friends of hers at her house. It was a delightful gathering. On the wall of the drawing room I saw a portrait of Mr. Worrall, which afforded me a longed-for reunion with him. Mrs. Worrall said, 'Two days before leaving for Japan, I talked with my husband. I was a bit afraid of going to Japan. Then he said, "I will go to Japan with you. You shall see the evidence of it there."' We talked about many things the description of which, I am afraid, would make my story too long. But finally let me add the following three things.

"First, my wife used to be extremely weak. She used to be a nurse when young. Therefore, paradoxically speaking, she doesn't trust doctors very much. I have often urged her to see a doctor, which she often did not obey. Frankly speaking, I have not urged her very strongly, either, because I was afraid that once she saw a doctor, she might be diagnosed to be seriously ill. She was wont to get tired and she was in bed for two days even after she had been shopping in Osaka which is about two hour round-trip train ride from our house. Such a weak person as she, after healed by Mrs. Worrall, could go to Europe and America which are much farther than Osaka.

"Secondly, frankly speaking, I had an impression that Mrs. Worrall was an ordinary lady. She was neither like a mysterious medium nor like a faultless saint. Hence, I recently came to have an ambition that I would like to have the same healing power as she through my effort and prayer because I could see the person whom others could not see after all. I considered it for a few days. Once I wondered what would happen if I could be endowed with such power. And I found out that I am, after all, such a person as cannot wholly escape from the temptation of making money with such power. I now realize that Mrs. Worrall is a wonderful lady who can carry out the message: 'When I preach the gospel, I may make the gospel without charge, so as not to use the full my right in the gospel' (I Corinthians 9:18).

"Thirdly, I am, of course, exceedingly delighted that I went through this experience. But as stated above, I have been proud that I am more like Thomas than Thomas himself. When I tell the story to people, some say, 'You have some peculiar power which others don't possess.' And others say, 'I wish I had such power.' To me these words sound either complimentary or cynical, but to them I reply thus. 'After that event, when I have a hundred students in my class, I am sometimes ridden with a fear that fifty of them are living people, while the other fifty may be mere ghosts.' As mentioned above, soon after the experience, I made some memoranda. And at the end of them, I wrote, 'I finish these memos with joy and fear.' I still feel the fear. Yet however great my fear may be, it is not great enough for me to forget the biblical passage: 'We cannot but speak the things which we saw and heard' (Acts 4:20)."

When I came to the end of Dr. Adachi's letter, Olga said, "Well?" and I knew what she meant. The sincerity of the man, the careful accuracy of his account, the eloquence of his presentation—all of these combined to convert the strange, incredible experience into something unforgettable, beautiful, and believable. I could understand completely why Olga had no doubt that Ambrose had kept his promise!

"I *am* entirely convinced that Ambrose was with me in Japan," she went on after a brief silence, as if she had read my mind, "and I do treasure Ambrose's communications to me for their personal worth—the love, the concern, and the help they give me in my everyday life. But the real significance of his message goes much deeper than all of this. They have provided me with a substantiation of much that I have come to believe from my psychic experiences; they have clarified and enlarged everything about the hereafter which I had previously glimpsed."

"You mean," I asked, "that Ambrose tells you specifics about his life as it is now—and about life there in general?"

"He does." Olga picked up the big notebook as she replied. "This is my careful record of what he has told me. When I go into the silence and he impresses his words upon my mind, I write them down while it is going on so that I won't make mistakes or forget. Do you want to go through all of this?"

Of course, I wanted to go through it, but I was too excited at the prospect to do more than nod in reply.

"Fine," said Olga. "Then take this home with you so you can have plenty of time. Ambrose has told me to let you have this material. He knows that you are beseiged by uncertanties and that you will read his messages without any surety even that they really are from him. But who knows? Maybe his voice will reach into your areas of unbelief where mine as yet hasn't."

Who could know? Was I one of those who could not "be persuaded, though one rose from the dead"? Or would Ambrose's voice from the dead enable me to say—as I had heard others before say with Emily Dickinson:

> I never spoke to God
> Nor visited in heaven;
> Yet certain am I of the spot
> As if the chart were given.

CHAPTER VIII

Beyond the Grave

THERE is something about the written word that is most impressive. Spoken thoughts, although beautiful or brilliant, flare up like fireworks: spectacularly but briefly. Ideas that are reduced to writing, however, are comparatively like images carved in stone: tangible and enduring. Unsurprisingly, therefore, while I admittedly had been fascinated by Olga Worrall's verbal psychic revelations, the written messages from Ambrose Worrall, purporting additionally to come from beyond the grave and confirming in great part what she had already said, were especially intriguing.

I began my examination of the manuscript that very day after I got back home. It was a very ordinary three-holed, looseleaf, black notebook—dime-store variety—filled with about one hundred fifty pages of written material. The first thing that I noticed in this superficial kind of perusal was that the signature at the end of each message was obviously done in a different handwriting from that used for the body of the message. Since this puzzled me, I promptly called Olga to find out "how-come."

"The writing," Olga explained over the telephone, "is mine. These communications are definitely *not* what is known as automatic writing. When I sit in the silence to talk to Ambrose, sometimes I ask questions and sometimes I just listen. In either case, I hear what he tells me with my inner ear, as if his words are impressing themselves on my mind, and I write everything down in my own handwriting. Then, whenever he is finished speaking and ready to say Goodbye, he takes my hand and signs his name just as he always used to sign it—with that fancy kind of an A and that formalized script which were uniquely his. The signature, therefore, is in Ambrose's handwriting; the rest is in mine."

After this clarification, I continued my study of the book. The papers were in chronological order with each new message headed simply by the date on which it was received. As I started to read the closely written sheets covered with writing in pencil on both sides, I became acutely aware of the specific nature of the overall communications: they were, in essence, love letters to a lonely wife from an absent husband who was conforting and assuring her of his constant affection and who was also attempting to give her as many details as possible of where he was and what he was doing and what it was all about.

In the early messages, as might be expected, the expressions of warmth and concern read like prose versions of Elizabeth Barrett Browning's famous "How Do I Love Thee?" sonnet.

"Darling", one 1972 page begins, "please don't cry. It makes it harder for me. Try to realize and sense my presence. We cannot do a thing about this separation other than wait. Honey, I'll try to do something physical to let you know I'm near you. Oh how I need you too. Your love sustains me until we are together again."

Another nearby page states: "Sweetheart, it is lonesome for me also but we have no choice and I am fortunate to be able to reach you in this way. I am with you. You will be pleased to know that I look good and feel well. Dearest, I will always be by your side. I love you more than ever—a new kind of love that is difficult to describe. Think of me as your invisible husband who loves you very, very much, and this I do and shall always. We are one. The spiritual aspects of our love endure forever. The physical is temporary, weak, undisciplined, to be forgotten, wiped away, to be regarded as an illusion. The real is the spiritual—lasting, forgiving, understanding, living for all eternity. This is our love, yours and mine. Give me your hand and your love as we continue our life together."

These declarations of love were intermingled with affectionate admonitions to Olga to get more rest, to secure help with domestic and outdoor chores, to attend particular social functions—Ambrose explaining his requests in these words: "I am still aware of things of the earth and I feel responsible to advise you." Intermingled, also, were sections forewarning Olga of the future events—alongside which, in bright ink, were notations made by her on subsequent dates to indicate when and how these prognostications came to pass; prognostications, incidentally, that were so uncomplicated and direct that they make those of Nostradamus sound more than ever like crossword puzzles.

The dominant theme of all the messages, though, was Ambrose's attempts to explain what the spirit world was like in particular. Initially, it appeared, any information along these lines was given by Ambrose in response to specific questions, but as the communications developed, unsolicited facts were offered in addition. Furthermore, with the passage of time, both the solicited and the unsolicited facts transmitted by Ambrose revealed his everincreasing intellectual and spiritual depth of understanding.

An early session, for example, during the nine o'clock silent time in which Olga asked specific questions, yielded comparatively simple and superficial answers. Olga's "What are you doing in the world of spirit?" elicited Ambrose's statement that he was doing the kind of work he had always done—helping those in need; that he worked through Olga each

Thursday at the New Life Clinic Healing Service; that he was being instructed in ways to improve the spiritual forces used in spiritual healing—a problem stemming from the difficulty involved in reducing spiritual energy to physical levels. Olga's next question "Is there a life before birth?" received the reply that the life spark begins at birth, from which point we develop and grow, and that there is not a life previous to this one. Olga's final question, composed of two main parts, "Do you find the spiritual world and you in it to be a duplicate of the physical world?" was answered by Ambrose in a rather generalized fashion: "The spirit world is the refined essence of the physical world. The entire system can be compared to an onion. Peel off the larger, denser layers one after another and you reach the heart or essence at the center. As for me, if you thought I was alive on earth, you ought to see me now!"

Other messages in the early stages give some of the basic facts of Ambrose's personal, everyday life in spirit. According to these, Ambrose had decided to base himself near Olga in their own home: "I am holding back somewhat," he said, "so I can be with you. Time enough for greater mental expansion after you join me." These messages speak also of being taken on a tour of the different realms of the vast world of spirit: "I have been visiting lovely gardens—flowers so fragrant and colors of every hue, many of which are unknown on earth. A fairy garden of posies! I have also attended many concerts—magnificent, beautiful music that you would have enjoyed. On some brief visits to higher levels which I have been shown as a preview of what advancement leads to, the music and colors are indescribable." There is even an account of a trip to the Spirit World Library: "Dearest, today I went to the Spirit World Library. What an experience! This is a place where psychometry is of great value. Through the touch, one can read a volume and receive the essence of a book's story. You will be good at it, as am I, but those who do not have this ability must learn other methods of perceiving."

As the pages of Olga's notebook turn, a complete picture of Ambrose's life in the spirit world emerges. Apparently he can dwell where he chooses, and there are new homes to be had as well as houses that have been vacated by those who have moved on to more advanced levels. Again and again, reference is made to conferences which he attends for learning purposes and to classes which he holds in order to teach others. He speaks frequently of experiments in big laboratories, of working with souls who need healing, and of happy times with many old friends and family members, most of whom he calls by name: "There are so many of our friends on this side of the pond and we get together and compare notes. Some of them look so much younger than I remembered that I could scarcely recognize them at first sight. Tom and Annie are together again. My mother sends her love to her other daughter—you."

Interesting as these personal messages are, they seem but to skim the surface of the richer knowledge about the world of spirit which later communications indicate Ambrose had begun to acquire. Repeatedly he complains about the inadequacy of our language to transmit for him new concepts, new places and new experiences which he is anxious to share—but he continues to try. In response to a question from Olga, for instance, he says:

"Where is the other world? Blended in this world the way the astral body is blended in the physical body: separate yet joined together. The atmosphere in the spirit world is finer and not as dense as it is on earth. Yet it is almost a duplicate of the earth world—except more advanced scientifically and, of course, spiritually. It is so difficult to explain! Life itself continues here, but with definite differences: we don't eat; we can transport our astral bodies by a thought or desire; we have no physical ailments, only mental ailments which we must learn to control. We love, we laugh, we weep for those we miss, and we can even be onery. Death does not confer sainthood on anyone and we must learn to master our emotions and thoughts for self-improvement and good mental health. Every opportunity for growth denied us on earth is available here, but only if we make the effort ourselves. One has but to ask sincerely and he will instantly be surrounded by willing helpers.

"You might say," Ambrose went on to conclude this session, "that our dimension is the mental counterpart of your dimension. Everything takes place here before it happens there. We are able to see earth's activities if we so choose—but you cannot see us. Still, this dimension is natural and normal. We absorb energy for our astral bodies; our minds are alert and indestructible and always will be: a spark of the Superior Mind, Intelligence, God—or call it what you will."

Another interesting communication that again refers to the inability to find suitable words with which to convey a new idea, is the following:

"Sweetheart, I wish I could really tell you all that goes on here. But how? Today, for example, I attended thought-creation classes. We call it 'higher dynamics' or force power—thought propulsion that can create an object or, in other words: think a thing and bring it into reality. As I've told you before, everything here is created by the power of mind. We think and then we project the idea in its entirety. On earth, man thinks, then transforms his thoughts to paper, shapes up a design, and finally builds. Not so here. We think things out and then create mentally. It takes much effort and study before results can be obtained so that a particular idea can be achieved in its entirety and not disintegrate before projection time. I even tried my hand at art-thinking, which means holding the thought of a color in mind long enough and skillfully enough to project it onto a canvas. This is truly a realm of great challenges! Do you see what I mean? There is so much I would like to tell you about my activities, but it is often impossible to reduce into words the unexplainable. I used to wonder why, when we would sit, our friends in spirit found it so difficult to answer all of our questions. Now the shoe is on my astral foot —and I understand."

With or without adequate language, however, Ambrose apparently maintained a continuing correspondence with Olga. He talks at times of being instructed in energy systems: "There are so many energy areas to learn about—which is not surprising, since all of life is movement. Take me, for example: I'm in your orbit; I occupy space with you; but I'm spinning so much faster than you are that you can't see me with your physical vision although we are actually side by side, just as we always were."

He refers, surprisingly—at least to me—in another message, to seances which, he says, are held in the spirit world in a fashion amazingly similar to those held here. His specific words are: "We even hold seances in our dimension in order to communicate with higher, more advanced souls. Our seances are preceded by periods of meditation in which we concentrate on what we need and seek from a higher source. Then we sit together in the silence so that we can receive answers to what we have asked."

He reports in several writings—apparently in response to Olga's requests for more physical manifestations—that it is very, very difficult to effect materializations. On one occasion, he says: "There are times when I'd love to do a physical manifestation but when I realize how much energy is needed, and you do not have physical mediumship, I have to be content to just kiss you even though you are not conscious of this effort on my part." On another occasion, he writes: "I'm making sounds for you"—Olga often told me of some loud, resounding noises that Ambrose frequently produces and I myself nearly flew out of my skin one night when I was at her house and a tremendous crash came from the dining-room buffet along-side me!—"but even these are not easy. I'm trying to learn how to do this without using too much of your physical energy. Every bit of physical manifestation can be produced only by using the energy of someone on earth. That is why physical mediums are such a help for any form of physical manifesta-tion, be it table-tilting, moving objects, producing materializa-tions, and so forth. The chemists on our side know how to manipulate the ectoplasm and energy taken from sitters to produce physical phenomena." On still another occasion, he laments: "Dearest, how I wish you had voice mediumship so that I could use this ability to speak to you! Instead, we must use this means of communication: projecting our thoughts to each other. I will try, though, to let you have more physical proof of my presence. It will be my present to you. I will ask some spirit friends for help. It is really only a veil of vibrations —motion, rates of speed—that keeps you from seeing me be-side you. In order for you to see me, I would have to slow down to your speed, which is much lower than mine. This can be done when conditions are favorable—except that they rarely are. Strong emotions, like grief, can help bring about such conditions—but I will try anyway."

Throughout all of Ambrose's messages, this note of frustra-tion over the separation of his world and Olga's and the diffi-culties involved in achieving complete communication re-sounds repeatedly like a major theme in a symphony. Fortunately, though, this frustration does not prevent his ren-dering some very interesting comments on spiritual healing which, in my opinion, are among the most significant points his communications make.

"Spiritual healing," he writes through Olga, "uses higher spiritual laws for physical healing. There are many levels of energy-outputs and many facets of these levels. In my level of being we deal with powers similar to electricity—and perhaps they do become electricity when they are toned down or reduced in frequencies on the earth level. Here these energies are extremely delicate and on a higher pitch or octave. Healers are on this pitch and healing energy flows through them to the patient. Still, this world and the physical world are one —only my side and the energies here are vibrating or oscillating on a higher octave. See? One piano but many octaves; yet one piano.

"I work in laboratories with many scientists whose work is concerned with our force fields and energies and ways in which they can be projected into your dimension. We use them here, you know, for many purposes, including healing. There are no physical ailments here but many people who are mind-sick. I am still primarily a healer because we carry our talents with us as we leave our bodies behind. There are so many here who need healing—those who take their physical ailments with them when they pass. They keep them in their minds and must be taught, therefore, how to drop these mental images of their earth illnesses. It is so very difficult to reach their minds but we all keep on trying to do what we can to help. Ever try to change a determined individual's thinking?

"It is so important that people be taught about this next place of life while still in the flesh. Then they can really leave their illnesses behind them along with their bodies and truly be whole and free to be born anew—to be perfect. When people come here unaware that life is continuing, it makes it hard for them and those who meet them. They refuse to accept the fact that they cannot return to their bodies. They insist that they are dreaming and they grow so upset because they cannot wake up to the dimension they left behind that they must be placed in rest homes and treated until they can accept the reality here."

Another communication from Ambrose offers the following comments: "I was with you today at the New Life Clinic.

There were many needy souls there from this dimension but they were unseen by human eyes. The healing service serves both sides. The prayers and healing thoughts of those present create a healing atmosphere that is effective and beneficial to those from our area, too.

"You are right, darling. As we both surmised, our astral bodies are perfect. Healing flows through the astral body into the physical body because the astral is attuned to a spiritual level of consciousness. While in the physical body and awake, we cannot see our astral bodies, which are not visible to physical sight but which are discernible to spiritual or clairvoyant vision. In spiritual healing, spiritual energy is absorbed by the astral body, which in turn passes it into the physical body and keeps it charged up—sort of like a battery charger. You know, the more I study here, the more I am becoming aware of the fact that spiritual healing is similar to electricity. One could call it paraelectricity.

"It is a force in healing that stimulates the sick cells and acts as a tonic to the cells, strengthening and helping them get back into their proper orbit—as they are off orbit when disturbed. This power works through the mind of the healer and is projected into the mind of the patient, from which it reaches the lowest level of the cells in the body where the need for healing is. Our bodies actually produce this type of energy constantly unless they are overworked or interfered with by wrong medication. Then a spiritual healer is needed to throw off—by touch or thought—the emergency switch that each body possesses and flips on when things are not going well. I know so little yet about the electrical components of the healing current! I am only a channel for it, just as an electric wire carries the power but is not the power. I keep studying and studying—so many of us in healing here look forward to the day when it can be harnessed by those on earth and directed when and where needed.

"I have been doing some experiments with instruments that

will soon be projected into a capable earth mind. The purpose is to produce a way to measure the size of our auric emanations and act as a detector for a person's state of health—narrow emanations would indicate a physical diminishing of energy and broader ones, going up on a scale, would mean the opposite. I've also attended some conferences recently—we don't really have your kind of time here—in which machinery was demonstrated. This machinery would be used to pick up human emanations to heal and bring mental harmony into lives. The main discussion centered on ways and means of sending into earth minds greater knowledge of inventions of a spiritual nature that will benefit all mankind. As of the moment, the real splendid truths we can project from here are received with distortion. But we have great expectations for what can someday be achieved."

This concern for the improvement of life on the physical level is recurrent throughout Ambrose's messages which deal with spiritual healing. Apparently, and interestingly, he feels that his healing ministry is still being continued on both sides of the Iron Curtain men call death: by him in the spirit world and by him in the physical world through Olga.

It comes clearly through that when Ambrose first passed on, his first communications to Olga revolved about the need for her to rest up and recover emotionally. Then he proceeded to urge her to carry on with their healing mission—and this last aspect of the messages in the black notebook emerges as the most meaningful of all.

"Dearest," he writes, not too long after he made the change, "you are very important to our ministry of long years of hard work. Our spirit friends—how odd to use that word now that I am one of them—anyway, they are busy making plans to further your ministry. I am busy also, consulting with experts on the various fields of forces and energies in healing so that I can project new knowledge to you. We call this mind expansion and you are a good subject to me because you are so receptive to my mind. Mind is indeed the powerhouse of the spirit.

"My hands are on your hands as you heal—now and always. We here in spirit are working through you for the glory of God and the spirit world."

Again and again, Ambrose keeps propelling Olga forward, plying her with endless instructions and encouragement much the way a loving mother does when she sends her only son off to the war. "Darling," a typical writing in this vein reads, "I worked with you today at the New Life Clinic. Many were touched. We are healing. Some of our friends on my side are developing a means of projecting still more healing energy through your hands. Now unlax. You shouldn't get so involved after the service because that is more tiring than the service itself. Just rest back and we will recharge you, dear. I cannot tell you how pleased I am and what a credit you are to our ministry."

Another such excerpt goes: "Dear One, your lecture today was excellent. You are doing a wonderful job—you are making a breakthrough for our long and hard struggle to bring spiritual healing in proper perspective to the forefront. You were receiving my thoughts perfectly even while you were talking. As I've told you before, we must have physical vehicles through which to work—carriers of our energy reduced to your level—slowing the 'vibes.' Remember? When you are rested, as you were this afternoon, I can get through to you so much more easily. This is a realm of mind. Sweetheart, the healing power is growing. Your gift coupled with mine has great strength.

"The interviews that you have been giving to the press take much time. I know. But it is your mission now not only to heal but also to make the world aware of God's power—to make people understand that we are all floating in his energy fields;

that when there is a short-circuit in our systems it shuts off the free flow of energy and it takes a spiritual healer to remove the short so that the body is working in all systems again. The only caution I want to give you is that you crowd your schedule too much—at least at times. Make room, though, for the scientists who will come to you to find out what spiritual healing is. Just concentrate on our ministry, beloved. I am with you always and our spirit friends will send all the helpers you need. They are all so pleased that you have stepped forward to carry on my ministry—ours—and that so much wonderful work can be performed through you. This is the time to spread the good word. Goodnight, dear. Sleep well and I'll see you in the astral."

This reference to an astral meeting is repeated frequently throughout all the messages. Ambrose talks of taking Olga with him to the spirit world; he reminds her of some of the fabulous gardens they saw together; he assures her that she is being strengthened and instructed for her healing work during these nightly, astral visits; he complains—but gently—during one session, that because she had been so exhausted the evening before from having overdone that day, he had been unable to have her accompany him into the astral: "You kept slipping back into the lower earth vibrations"; and he even exults when she can remember some of her astral trips with him afterward. "Don't worry about not recalling all we do. Just know that I take you with me when you leave your body asleep. Soon you will begin to recall more—and you did remember a bit of our last visit today. Good girl!"

When, finally, I had finished reading the entire manuscript —which was a matter of several days—I telephoned Olga and stopped by her house to return it.

"Well," she greeted me, as I handed her the notebook, "did you get through it all?"

"All," I affirmed.

"And what do you think?" she asked eagerly.

"I don't know what to think," I confessed. "It's utterly incredible!"

"It is," she agreed. Then she began quizzing me as if to help ascertain my reaction. "Did you notice that when I asked what the purpose of life was, he said he didn't know—that no one on his level, apparently, knew, either—that he was not advanced enough yet for such understanding?"

"I did notice that particularly," I replied, "because if there's anything I'd like to find out, it's exactly that. Why? What for? He only says"—and I took the book back to find the right place —"'We must arise and grow spiritually. We all make mistakes because of ignorance of the true values of life. This is man's weakness. The new life gives us every opportunity to look back and then correct by whatever means possible the foolish things we did.'"

Olga sighed appreciatively. Then she continued, "And did you notice his answer when I asked him why he had to go from me so soon?"

"I did," I exclaimed. "It was so unusual and interesting." I flipped pages again, but with greater ease this time, because I had marked this place. "I put a clip here because I meant to ask you about it. He says, 'Honey, I had to leave as I told you. I used up all the heartbeats. Yes, dear. Our bodies in forming acquire genetic life from our ancestors—long or short or middle.'" I looked up at Olga. "How does that strike you?"

"Just as it does you," she laughed. "Edwina child, I only get these messages from Ambrose. I don't edit or argue with what he says—but I do find them fascinating. A great deal, though, is not very new to me—it just verifies what he and I had both learned on some of our astral trips before he made the change. For instance, take his statement that every kind of religion practiced in earth is available in the spirit world, except that some of the basic thinking has to be changed. He says that like attracts like: people who wish to follow the same circle of repeated words and motions, even though they find themselves in spirit in an environment contrary to what they had been taught to believe, find others of a similar nature there and together maintain their status quo until, sooner or later, a stirring occurs in their souls which makes them break the hypnotic spell of reiteration and start on the path of spiritual progress."

"You've just reminded me of another thing," I said, when Olga finished speaking. "The messages constantly refer to your astral travels with Ambrose—almost every night. Is that so? Do you do that?"

"That's what he tells me," Olga replied.

"Do you remember any of it?" I asked with great curiosity.

"Some." Olga was obviously trying to be extremely accurate. "Actually, I keep remembering more as time goes on. Ambrose did say that this would take place gradually—and it is beginning to do so. Some mornings when I awake, I recollect nothing. Some mornings, I can't remember anything specific, but I have a general awareness that I have been in the astral. Just occasional mornings—too few, unfortunately—I can actually recall what happened while I presumably slept."

"What an exciting thing it must be when you can retain such an experience!" I said. "That would be really making contact in a personal and direct way. That's what everyone who has lost a loved one wants."

"They want it over there, too," Olga pointed out to me. "From time to time Ambrose speaks of classes he holds for people who want to learn how to reach out of the world of spirit and communicate with their families or friends here. If you can perceive them mentally—the same as you and me— then you can begin to imagine that it might be just as frustrating to them when we can't see or hear them whenever they are near and trying to get our attention."

I did remember several passages to this effect; and now it was my turn to sigh. "Olga," I said, closing the book and giving it back to her again, "I will admit that I am very much impressed with Ambrose's communications. Somehow, though, I feel now as if I have been swimming way out into the middle of a huge ocean where there is nothing but water all around me and no longer anything solid on which to rest. Ambrose sounds so real, so alive in these writings. He does. Yet I know he isn't alive—at least, in our sense."

"But that's just it!" Olga countered. "He is alive in *every* sense of the word. Don't you see it at all? Why do you think I have let you read these pages when I know what most people would think of anyone who professes to talk with someone who isn't visibly there? Why do you think Ambrose told me to give you the notebook—which he did. Because it is our God-given responsibility—and these are his words—'to give comfort and understanding to all who are crying out for assurance that life continues.' Of course, there are many who believe; but when we add knowledge to faith, we are invincible."

Looking into Olga's shining eyes, I glimpsed her own feeling of invincibility. Whether I did or did not understand, whether others would or would not be persuaded, Ambrose's voice from beyond the grave had given Olga her final, full measure of conviction. There could be no doubt, as of now, that for her, death had been swallowed up in victory; the grave had no more sting.

CHAPTER IX

On the Psychic Witness Stand

THIS is the space age, with all the connotations that these words can hold. We are rooted in the earth and we reach for the stars. We talk of God and we worship science. We analyze, experiment, and probe into every aspect of human life from sex to moon particles in a mammoth effort to dissect it all and lay it out on neat slides under our microscopic lenses. By logical extension, therefore, we have carried this clinical approach into the world of the occult as well—and I was not even slightly surprised to discover that Olga Worrall had been a frequent guinea pig in this universal laboratory.

It was actually on the very same day on which I returned Olga's notebook filled with Ambrose's communications that the subject of scientific investigation of the psychic came up. Olga had gone over to one of her filing cabinets to put the manuscript away and had pulled open the wrong drawer, apparently, for she grimaced at herself and said: "Ugh! I almost misplaced this. That's what I get for keeping such late hours."

"Why were you up so late?" I asked. "What were you doing?"

"Conducting an experiment with Bob Miller," she glibly answered. "He from his end down in Georgia and I, from up here in Baltimore. It was exciting but a real challenge."

"What kind of experiment are you talking about?" I was honestly puzzled, promptly conjuring up in my mind a kind of Frankenstein version of an atomic laboratory: boiling flasks, bulging testtubes, and white-coated chemists. How on earth did Olga fit into any of that?

She didn't, of course. "I'm talking about mental experiments," she explained, as if she had realized what I was thinking. "Dr. Miller—he's got a Ph.D. in one of the sciences—is doing tests to see if we can obtain objective proof of the power of mind and if we can possibly register concrete evidence of spiritual healing. Haven't I mentioned any of this to you before?"

"Never," I declared emphatically.

"Well," she began, "better late than never. Now where to begin?" She paused for a moment and then searched through a few files until she came up with a big batch of papers. "You know Ambrose was an engineer?" I nodded. "As an engineer," she then continued, "he always looked forward to the day when scientists would be able to prove that spiritual and mental forces not only exist but have great power. He used to say" —and she quoted from memory—"'By following the scientific method and using scientists who are not limited by material concepts it should be possible to learn something of the world beyond the physical limitations of this world in a way that would be acceptable to science.'"

"You mean prove the unprovable?" I countered, openly skeptical.

"If you can prove it," Olga replied, "then it's no longer unprovable."

"But how can you possibly do that?" I insisted.

"I didn't say it was easy," Olga conceded. "Nevertheless, both Ambrose and I cooperated with doctors, parapsychologists, and all kinds of scientists who were interested in examining the paranormal. Now that I am here alone, I have gone on with this aspect of our work—at Ambrose's special urging," she added. "Didn't you notice the many times he tells me to do this in the messages?"

"I definitely recall many references to that effect," I admitted, "But I didn't take it literally at all."

"It was meant literally," Olga told me. "Years ago, even, we would have all sorts of investigators come to our home, especially on weekends when Ambrose was free."

"What could they do in your house?" I asked, still clinging to my Medical Center vision.

"Oh, lots of things," Olga answered.

She then elaborated on some of the specific testing that was done. Apparently the investigators would arrive with their instruments and electronic equipment in tow. In one series of experiments, for example, Ambrose and Olga would each independently hold various rods and wires in their hands, which rods and wires were attached to other machines so that the flow of energy from their hands could be measured.

"This," she remembered, "was done to see if an excessive flow of energy does emerge from a healer's hands—and how much when spiritual healing by the laying-on of hands is in progress. And according to those tests, it definitely does."

On another occasion, Olga told me, a group of scientists set up a breadboard version of some electronic equipment in the Worrall basement to see if Olga could detect sound that could not be heard by the human ear. She was not informed of the nature of this experiment, only told to keep quiet and tell them whenever she received some kind of impression—any kind at all. Whereupon, she sat obediently silent for quite a while, merely observing the little mouse on the table in a cage and the men who kept turning the dials on the equipment. Suddenly, Olga announced that they were at 44,000 cycles and that this was affecting the mouse.

"The moment I said that," Olga smiled at the memory, "it

was absolute pandemonium. Several minutes elapsed while the men checked the calculations to make an accurate reading. Then one of them shrieked, 'My God! She's right. It's exactly at forty-four thousand!' And the one lawyer present— he had been brought by one of the doctors—said, 'This place is spooky! How could she know? I'm leaving!' and he ran out."

I laughed with Olga at the picture she had painted. Then I asked her what the objective of the test had been.

"Honey," Olga declared, "I'm not one for science. That was Ambrose's field. I merely cooperate as they ask me. I think what they were getting at that time was something to do with finding out what level of unheard sound could affect mice with tumors and if any healing could be achieved through such effects."

As Olga talked and talked—obviously enjoying the reminiscing—I began to realize the broad scope of the scientific experimentation with which she and Ambrose had been involved for many years. There had been tests designed to verify their psychometric ability by concealing chemicals in packages or flasks which Olga and Ambrose were instructed to hold.

"We were always able to name the concealed chemicals," Olga reported to me. "Once, I remember, I not only knew that the package I was holding contained iodine, but I had a distinct taste of iodine in my mouth."

There were other tests directed to measuring the extent of their clairvoyant abilities: they were taken into laboratories and asked to give their impressions of the test animals.

"I'll never forget the time," Olga said, "when a researcher, a medical doctor, brought some bottles to our home in which he had placed the fur of some animals he was working with. We told him—in connection with one particular flask—that we were 'getting oats' with that one and that the animals who were supposed to be on a starvation diet were actually absorb-

ing the 'essence' of the oats. The shocked doctor declared that
he did indeed have a bag of oats right next to the cage and he
had been puzzled because the animals were not responding to
a starvation diet. We couldn't—any more than he—explain
how such absorption could take place, but if we can become
ill by absorbing chemicals in the air without even knowing
what is happening, then who can say that animals can't absorb
whatever is given off by oat seeds?"

There were more structured, formalized tests, as well, and
for these Olga possessed documented and officially signed papers attesting to the facts. Both Ambrose and Olga, for example, attended many sessions at Wainwright House, a seminar
center in New York state, where members of the professions,
including clergymen, and laymen gather periodically to in-
quire into spiritual healing. In some of the experiments that
were held there, qualified and interested physicians sought to
measure by instruments the energy output of persons doing
spiritual healing. When Ambrose was tested before the healing session began, it was found that his energy level was low.
During the healing session, his energy level increased way
beyond the level ever before recorded by anyone with the use
of this equipment. After the healing session, the energy level
remained much above normal—and the same pattern was
shown by the patient; low before, greatly increased during
treatment, and still high afterward.

"Do you remember," Olga reminded me in an aside, while
she was relating this, "that I told you that I always feel energized *after* a healing session? Those tests show why."

Many experimental sessions were held at Wainwright
House over the years. On one occasion Ambrose was able to
slow down a watch by magnetizing it with his thought: specifically, looking at it with concentration for a few moments.
There were a number of observers present, all of whom noted
the deceleration. Another time, when X-ray film was placed

on the palms of Olga's and Ambrose's hands, the subsequently developed film showed an unexplainable, strange white line running across it. Although this phenomenon was repeated, none of the scientists present could even begin to speculate on the occurrence.

"These are fascinating tests," I told Olga when she paused for breath, "but what are they supposed to mean?"

"Well, look at it this way," Olga replied patiently. "Most skeptics, for instance, say that spiritual healing is pure emotionalism or psychological effects. If we can demonstrate, though, as Ambrose and I often have, that there is a heightened energy that comes from a healer's hands—don't you think that this means something? Also, if we can demonstrate clairvoyance and ESP in a valid way, surely that must indicate that such things exist as realities and not just as figments of a witch's cauldron."

This logic seemed sound enough and I settled back again against the sofa pillows to listen some more. Olga, meanwhile, was rummaging through her papers, as if in search of some special items, until she apparently found what she wanted.

"Here's an interesting one," she exclaimed, pulling out the pertinent page and reading it aloud: "In 1967 Dr. Robert Miller directed an experiment to determine if prayer can have beneficial effect on remotely located plants. The growth rate of rye grass was measured to an accuracy of 1.0 mil per hour by means of a mechanical, electrical transducer which was attached to a blade of grass through a lever arm.

"On January fourth, 1967, in Atlanta, Georgia, the growth of a new blade of rye grass had been stabilized at six mils per hours. At eight P.M., a telephone call had been made to Ambrose and Olga Worrall in Baltimore, Maryland, asking them to pray for the plant, which was the subject of the experiment, during their nine P.M. silent time. The Worralls agreed to do so, and at nine P.M., as per this request, they employed the following method of prayer on behalf of the plant: they visualized it as growing vigorously under ideal conditions.

"The next morning, observations were made from the trace on the strip-chart recorder. It was found that before the prayer was begun, the trace was a straight line with a slope showing a growth rate of 6.25 mils per hour. At nine P.M. sharp, the trace began to deviate upwards and by eight A.M., the following morning, the growth rate was 52.5 mils per hour —an increase of 830 percent. The plot was then continued for forty-eight hours more, during which time the growth rate decreased but never returned to the original rate.

"During the entire period of this experiment, the door of the room in which the plant was housed was kept locked; the temperature was constantly maintained at seventy to seventy-two degrees farenheit; the fluorescent lights were turned continuously on. There was clearly no known variable which could cause such a dramatic increase in growth rate of the rye grass. Wherefore, these facts would indicate that Ambrose and Olga Worrall, six hundred miles away, had been able to cause an eightfold increase in a plant's growth rate simply by concentrating their thoughts on the plant and by doing so for less than five minutes in all."

When Olga finished reading this written statement of Dr. Miller's account, she looked up at me with an enigmatic smile. "Interesting?" she asked.

"Very interesting," I agreed.

"Especially," she pointed out, "when you realize that this experiment was undertaken and completed successfully way before any of the business about loving plants, et cetera, ever became popularized; and it was done at a great distance. The significance of it all, though, is the fact that this type of test proves that something more than just words happens when you pray—that prayer has physical force and physical results."

In the brief silence which followed this evaluation, another thought came into my mind. "What you've been telling me, Olga," I said, "is what you and Ambrose have done together over the years. Have you gone on with this yourself without Ambrose—and how good have your results been?"

"They've been marvelous." Olga absolutely beamed. "But I haven't really been doing things *without* Ambrose. I assure you he has helped me up and down the line. He keeps saying so in his messages, you know—or didn't you take that literally either?"

I laughed guiltily in reply and Olga laughed also. "Oh, ye of little faith!" she groaned. Then she continued very seriously: "Actually, the scientific interest in my work has grown tremendously. Since that *Medical Economics* article, for instance, I have had doctors write to me from coast to coast; and they've even come for healing and to talk to the New Life Clinic. They've also referred patients for help and are tracking the results.

"But most important of all are the organized groups that are investigating paranormal healing these days—for whom I have lectured and given healing demonstrations and submitted to carefully controlled experimentation. Take my visit to Japan in March to May of 1973 as an illustration. When I visited Japan, I was asked by Dr. Heroshi Motoyama of the Institute for Religious Psychology in Tokyo to participate in some tests in his laboratory. I agreed and went with some friends, my host, Dr. Bray, and the dean of a nearby college to Dr. Motoyama's lab. In this room, which was filled with my group, five of Dr. Motoyama's assistants, and various types of complex, electronic equipment, alligator clips with wires were attached to my fingers and also to some machinery. The measurements that were being recorded had to be repeated five times, according to Dr. Motoyama, in order to be scientifically acceptable.

"After five runs, I was asked to go into a 'healing mood' so that a new series of measurements could be made. When I told Dr. Motoyama that I could not just do this, but that I needed someone in need of healing to trigger off the flow of healing energy, one gentleman stepped forward and asked me to help him. In a flash, I perceived his illness, informed him of the diagnosis—which merely confirmed what his doctor had already told him—and proceeded with the laying-on of hands. Throughout the treatment, the equipment was being operated by Dr. Motoyama, who afterward announced that the machines registered an unusual amount of energy flowing from my hands—a greater flow than he had ever before measured from anyone."

Since this seemed to conclude this account, I could not resist asking, "And what about the patient?"

Olga burst out laughing. "You're completely right," she declared. "First things first—but that's what happens when you get so busy trying to prove what you're doing that you almost forget why you're doing it. Actually, it was a superb healing demonstration. The patient said he felt great heat from my hands and, by later report, I learned that he had been healed, and two bystanders in the laboratory had been healed at the same time."

At this point Olga gave me a sheet of paper to read. "Why don't you glance through this?" she suggested. "You know how scientific things confuse me. But this is Dr. Motoyama's own statement about the tests he conducted. It's concise and clear and it won't take you more than a few minutes to look at."

Dr. Motoyama's report, which I then read, went as follows:

"Olga Worrall, famous American Spiritual healer, came to the Institute of Religious Psychology at the invitation of Dr. Hiroshi Motoyama, Director. Mrs. Worrall was in Japan under the auspices of the Methodist Mission and had been conducting healing workshops and services in churches throughout the Tokyo and Osaka areas.

"Dr. Motoyama had met Mrs. Worrall in Little Rock, Arkansas, last June when both were speakers at the Annual Conference of the ESP Research Associates Foundation, an organization founded by Dr. Harold Sherman for those interested in psychic phenomena. Dr. Sherman had suggested that Dr. Motoyama test Mrs. Worrall's psi ability during her visit to Japan with his unique electronic apparatus incorporating a computer. This was successfully accomplished, and the group, which included Professor William Bray and Professor Kenneth Dale, who accompanied Mrs. Worrall, joined Dr. and Mrs. Motoyama for lunch.

"Dr. Motoyama gave the results concerning Mrs. Worrall's psi ability as follows: One characteristic belonging to the psychic person is standard deviation of skin current of the 28 meridian (seiketsu) points which is very high compared with the ordinary person. For instance, in the average person the value is from 0.1 to 0.26, but Mrs. Worrall showed 1.0, a very much higher value, which means that Mrs. Worrall is a psychic person. Then after comparison between readings before and during faith healing through her hands and fingers, meridians of the left-hand fingers showed a high significant difference between before and during faith healing.

"Consequently, we can infer that her psi ability is more easily projected from the left as compared to the right hand. The meridians which showed significant difference are of the genito-urinary system, the digestive system, and the heart circulatory system, which, according to the yoga chakra system, means in her case that the anahata, manipura and vishuda chakras are predominently working."

While I was reading this material, Olga was busy finding other things for me to see. "Have I ever shown you any of these test photographs?" she finally said, producing some pictures from her file. "I didn't think so," she went on as I said No. "Let me explain these. Last year I was in California lecturing for the Academy of Parapsychology and Medicine. During my stay, I did some tests for Dr. Thelma Moss—"

"Who is she?" I interrupted.

"Dr. Moss is a medical psychologist and an assistant professor at UCLA's Neuropsychiatric Institute," Olga replied. "Her primary interest is in parapsychology and psychical research, although I understand that she does teach a course in parapsychology at UCLA. Anyway, we did some tests using Kirlian photography—that new kind of photography that shows the electrical energy in a thing, almost like getting the aura. Dr. Moss took a leaf and snapped it as it appeared on the plant. Then she damaged it severely by cutting part of it away—and she took a Kirlian photograph of that. I was then asked to hold the leaf in my hand and administer spiritual healing—after which the leaf was again photographed. When the leaf pictures were compared, it was glaringly obvious that the damaged leaf was being repaired—sort of reconstituted—by the healing treatment. Here," Olga abruptly concluded, "see for yourself."

The photographs—properly attested—were indeed amazing. I could easily see the normal leaf configuration in the first, the big gap and duller overall pattern in the second print of the damaged leaf, and the filling-in and startling brightness of the same leaf after healing.

"Isn't it something?" Olga asked enthusiastically, before I could say a word. "Now look at these four photos—Kirlian also —of my fingertips: resting, beginning a healing, in the middle of a healing, and immediately after a healing."

I saw in the first shot a faint outline, dimly bright, of a fingertip. As healing was undertaken, however, the brightness outlining the fingertip increased not only in brilliance but went from a thin-line dimension to something measuring about one quarter of an inch wide by the time the healing was at its height—each succeeding print demonstrating a gradual enlargement which was maintained afterward.

Again, when I finished my examination, Olga gave me no opportunity to speak. "Aren't these exciting!" she exclaimed with obvious delight. "Not only do these prove that during a healing the coronas are greatly increased, but they also show that the increase remains—at least for a while, and, repeatedly with the same results, the patient's fingertips registered in the same way."

She paused finally and I managed to say, "These are really exciting—sort of black-and-white, objective evidence that something seems to actually happen in the healing process."

"Exactly," Olga confirmed. "I've participated in many tests designed to establish this principle, but nothing has ever set it forth so dramatically and so vividly as these photographs."

"Probably so," I agreed, "but what other kinds of tests are there? I mean," I explained, "in addition to some of these electrical ones you've already mentioned."

"Oh, several kinds," Olga responded quickly. "For example, I've worked with Sister Justa Smith when she was associated with Rosary Hill College. She had me hold, in healing, enzymes, whole blood, serum, tap water, and distilled water to see if my touch on the different vials affected them. Kirlian photographs were taken of the specimens before testing—for control purposes—and after I had administered the healing touch, and the results showed that the specimens were affected.

"Another time I was asked by Dr. Makari, a friend of Ambrose's and mine, to do a long-distance experiment with him. The purpose was to make a muscle of a pig's uterus quiver in a particular way by concentrating on it from Baltimore while the specimen was in New Jersey. After conditions were stabilized in the laboratory, he telephoned and I visualized the muscle responding to my thought. This was done twice, and each time the muscle quivered at the precise time we concentrated on it.

"There was even some kind of Life Force Test that I took part in once, also," and Olga began searching among her papers as she mentioned this particular experiment. "It involved treated live yeast cells and—"

She broke off suddenly as she apparently found the pertinent paper. "Here," she said, "you read it for yourself."

The paper she gave me was headed "Life Force Test" and read:

"The test in which you participated measures the amount of healing energy induced into the treated linen by your hands and thoughts. Before you held the cloth it had been treated with live yeast cells and the enzyme 'Zymase.' After you energized the cloth it was placed in a nutrient solution and the vitality of the yeast cells was measured. The result is a direct indication of your healing energy.

"The result of your test is rated on a scale of 1 to 10. It should be understood that only one percent of those tested will rate 10.

"ANY RATING OVER 4 IS VERY GOOD—AND RATINGS OF 1 OR MORE INDICATE ENERGY THAT CAN BE USED SUCCESSFULLY.

Your Rating
0   1   2   3   4   5   6   7   8   9   <u>10</u>"

This report was signed C. Moody, Director PSI Research.

"Honey," Olga sighed, as I looked up again, "I've been tested so much, I can't even remember it all. And why should I?" she said, suddenly beginning to laugh. "After all, I'm not the one who needs convincing."

I joined in her laughter. Then I asked, "Do you have any particular experiment that you think has especial significance?"

"Not really," Olga spoke reflectively. "They're all little pebbles pointing the way. But I do feel that all the distance tests are very important, since so much of the healing work I do is distance healing. In this vein, if we can demonstrate that things can be accomplished by me when I am far removed from the object to be acted upon, we are establishing a major point."

I could see that. "Have you done any specific distance tests recently?"

"Have I!" Olga exclaimed with a big smile. "Maybe I've been saving the best for last. Seriously, though, I have done a very exciting distance test just a couple of months ago. It was for Dr. Robert Miller, the man I mentioned before. Remember? Ambrose and I did the distance prayer on plants for him. But first, let me tell you a little about how it all came to pass."

In January of 1974, Olga apparently flew down to Atlanta to give some lectures at Agnes Scott College—the college where Dr. Miller does not teach, but conducts research. One full day on campus was devoted to experiments with an Atlanta research group which includes scientists, professors, engineers, nurses, and medical technicians, and which is headed by Dr. Miller and Dr. Phil Reinhart of the college physics department.

As Olga tells it: "There were different types of tests. We worked in the physics laboratory. In one test, a piece of my jewelry was placed under a can, with two similar cans, making all three alike. The person who hid the jewelry left the room. I was brought into the room by several persons, one of them the college psychologist, making sure I did not get any help from anyone. I was given a pair of dowsing rods to work with, but before I touched the rods I 'knew' where the jewelry was, and pointed to the right can.

"This was done three times and each time I 'found' the jewelry. I located water in the room, really an underground stream. I was taken into the photographic dark room, and handed some rocks to see if I could detect any emanations. I described to the man with me exactly what I 'saw.' With great excitement the men informed me that a scientist in about 1850 working with a sensitive obtained the same results. A most important test involved the cloud chamber. I was asked to place my hands around a cloud chamber, the energy flow from my hands disturbed the cloud chamber and it became turbulant. There were at least nine persons in the lab who attempted to disturb the cloud chamber without results, yet when I placed my hands around the chamber there was activity. I was asked to energize some water. It was used on salt crystals. Tap water was used on the control. My crystals changed color from the normal color always observed with ordinary water. The magnetized water was tested and its viscosity was altered, as well as its electrical properties, so the scientist informed me.

"As you can imagine," Olga concluded this recital, "it was a busy and hectic but rewarding session. The cloud-chamber part of it, though, seemed to be the one that attracted the most attention. So much so, that Dr. Miller called me after I got back home and asked me if I would participate in a long-distance test to affect the cloud chamber. I immediately agreed to do this and the time was then set. When I projected myself astrally, I went into the lab where I had been before. However, I found the lab empty and had to locate the proper lab, which I did very quickly. The room had a very long table with the cloud chamber at one end. In the room, besides Miller and Reinhart, were two extra persons in the corner of the room, projecting the thought that the experiment be successful. Their broadcasting interfered with me so I had to 'shut them out,' and then proceed with the experiment. This took about five minutes for the test. Then I 'returned back to my physical body.' The phone rang shortly after to inform me that I did cause the chamber to become turbulent. I told Dr. Miller that I had to locate the right lab and he laughed and said that he had decided to change labs, but he forgot to tell me. I also told him about the two extra persons, and I was right and they were indeed broadcasting the thought of success. The men asked if I would try to repeat the experiment. I agreed, so about fifteen minutes later they phoned to say they were ready. I again did my 'stuff,' and again the chamber responded."

Throughout this presentation, one question was dominant in my mind. The moment Olga stopped talking, therefore, I asked, "What is a cloud chamber?"

Olga burst out laughing. "Edwina," she declared, "you're as bad as I am. Look, here's a copy of Dr. Miller's official write-up of the experiment which he's just put together for the *Science of Mind* magazine. It's a lot more scientific than I could ever hope to be. Why don't you read this for yourself while I play Gunga Din and go get us some iced tea?"

With this, she stood up, gave me a few typewritten pages, and left the room. In a matter of seconds, thereafter, I was completely immersed in Dr. Miller's report, entitled "Scientists Register Thought Energy", co-authored by Dr. Robert N. Miller, Dr. Philip B. Reinhart, and Anita Kern. The exact text follows:

"A potentially powerful tool for research in the field of thought as energy was discovered when Dr. Olga Worrall, internationally known spiritual healer, participated in a series of experiments with the authors. The investigators were Dr. Robert N. Miller, a former Georgia Tech Professor, who is now an industrial research scientist; Dr. Philip B. Reinhart, Head of the Physics Department of Agnes Scott College; and Anita Kern, a senior and physics major at Agnes Scott. The research was conducted under the auspices of the Ernest Holmes Research Foundation.

"Dr. Worrall visited Agnes Scott College in Atlanta, Georgia, during January of 1974 to address students, faculty, and visitors. One full day was devoted to paraphysical tests, which were conducted in the physics laboratory. The key experiment had the objective of determining whether or not some type of measurable energy is given off by a healer's hands. A cloud chamber, an apparatus originally developed by nuclear physicists for making visible the path of high energy nuclear particles, was used as the detector.

"The Atomic Laboratories' Model 71850 cloud chamber was used in the experiment. It consists of a cylindrical glass chamber seven inches in diameter and five inches in height, which has a sheet aluminum bottom and a viewing glass across the top. The unit is operated by covering the floor of the chamber with a ¼" layer of methyl alcohol and placing the entire unit upon a flat block of dry ice.

"When the liquid surface of the alcohol is in contact with a closed volume of air, some of the molecules of the liquid evaporate into the air to form a vapor. Equilibrium conditions are reached when the rate of evaporation from the liquid surface is just balanced by the rate of re-entry of the alcohol molecules from the vapor state into the liquid.

"When the bottom of the chamber is chilled by the dry ice, a supersaturated zone about one inch in height is created in the chamber. Condensation in the form of a mist then occurs. A charged particle, such as an alpha or beta particle, in passing through the chamber ionizes molecules of air and vapor and produces a trail of positive and negative ions along its path. The alcohol vapor preferentially condenses on these nuclei and a visible trail of droplets is formed. A spotlight mounted at the side of the chamber provides the lighting necessary for photographing the tracks.

"During the experiment Dr. Worrall placed her hands at the side of the cloud chamber without touching the glass. She then visualized energy flowing from her hands, much as she does when treating a patient. The observers saw a wave pattern develop in the mist of the sensitive zone, which, until she placed her hands in position, had been quite uniform in appearance. The waves were parallel to her hands and the apparent direction of motion was perpendicular to the palms.

"After several minutes Dr. Worrall shifted her position 90 degrees to see if the pattern in the cloud chamber would be affected. The waves began to change direction and were soon moving perpendicular to their original path. Unfortunately, no camera had been set up for the experiment and a photographic record was not obtained.

"On March 12, 1974, a follow-up experiment was conducted. In this experiment a camera was mounted so as to enable photographs of the cloud chamber activity to be made. In addition, the experiment was designed to determine if Mrs. Worrall could affect the cloud chamber at a distance. To achieve this result the cloud chamber was in the physics laboratory at Agnes Scott College in Atlanta, Georgia, but Olga Worrall remained in Baltimore, Maryland, some 600 miles away.

"After the cloud chamber had attained a steady state condition, a telephone call was made to Baltimore to let Dr. Worrall know that all was in order and to ask her if at 8:50 P.M. she would concentrate her thoughts and energies upon the cloud chamber. It was suggested that she mentally hold her hands at the sides of the chamber for several minutes and then change the orientation 90 degrees as she did when she was actually present in the physics laboratory.

"Just before the telephone call was made, the sensitivity of the cloud chamber was checked by inserting a radium 226 alpha source into the chamber and observing the condensed vapor trails generated by the alpha particles. A photograph was taken at that time. Except for the alpha tracks only a fine mist, uniformly distributed, was visible. At 8:53 a definite change occurred in the cloud chamber. The mist began to pulsate and dark waves were visible in the chamber. The waves were parallel to the long direction of the table. The pulsation continued for about seven minutes but never changed direction. Then the motion in the chamber gradually subsided.

"At 9:10 P.M. a second telephone call was made to get Dr. Worrall's report of her mental impressions. She said she had been able to transfer her consciousness to the laboratory and then she mentally placed her hands at the sides of the chamber and focused her attention on producing motion in the chamber. She felt a cool sensation as if a cold breeze was flowing over her hands. She also said that she did not shift the position of her hands during the experiment. This explains why the wave pattern did not change direction.

"The two scientists discussed the experiment after the telephone conversation was completed, and Dr. Reinhart commented that it would be even more conclusive if the experiment could be repeated. Since the cloud chamber was already operating and stabilized, it was decided to call Mrs. Worrall and ask if she would again concentrate on the cloud chamber.

"The experiment was repeated and the sensitive zone of the chamber again became turbulent, and undulations at the rate of about one per second were perceived. Photographs were taken of the interior of the cloud chamber before, during, and after the second experiment. A time interval of approximately eight minutes was required for the turbulence to subside after the second test.

"In a final telephone conversation, Dr. Worrall, Dr. Reinhart, and Mr. Miller discussed the time interval required for the sensitive zone of the chamber to become quiescent after each experiment. Mr. Worrall suggested that the cloud chamber had become charged with some type of energy and a finite time was required for its dissipation.

"This statement raises such questions as what kind of energy is involved and why does it create turbulence in a cloud chamber when it is introduced or while it dissipates? Dr. Worrall also said that, both in local and distant healing, the energy acts much as it did in the cloud chamber; it churns up activity and stimulates cell action.

"The experiment appears to be repeatable. However, because of the limited number of tests conducted, the possibility of coincidences and extraneous influences cannot be entirely ruled out. Additional experiments under still more vigorously controlled conditions are now being conducted to establish statistical validity.

"In summary, through the use of the cloud chamber, a recognized and accepted research tool, the theory that a tangible energy issues from the hands of healers is given support. A change in the cloud chamber pattern resulted when Mrs. Worrall held her hands around the chamber. Other members of the investigating team placed their hands around the chamber with no results. The results of the second experiment, in which she was 600 miles away from the cloud chamber, indicate that 'thoughts are things' and visible manifestations in the physical world can be produced mentally from a distance."

By the time I reached the end of Dr. Miller's report, Olga was back in the room with a small tray and two tall glasses of iced tea.

"Any comment?" she asked, as I took the proferred glass. "Or are you going to plead the Fifth Amendment?"

She laughed at her own little joke and I laughed, too. Then I answered, "What comment could I possibly make? All of these tests are impressive—especially this statement I've just read. But what does it really mean? This cloud-chamber test, for example. What does it prove?"

"It proves only what a person is willing to let it prove," Olga replied. "For me, at the very least, when I can affect a cloud chamber six hundred miles away from where I am, it proves, as Dr. Miller put it"—and she took the paper from my hand to read aloud—"'. . . thoughts are things and visible manifestations in the physical world can be produced mentally from a distance.'"

"But does that prove," I persisted, "that spiritual healing can be accomplished at a distance? In other words, can you extend the turbulence in a cloud chamber to the whole concept of spiritual healing? And by the same token, can you extend the demonstrable, unusual energy emanating from your hands to the establishment of the fact of healing itself?"

Olga smiled at me ruefully. "Perhaps *you* can't," she answered, "but many can. How can anything like spiritual healing or clairvoyance be proved conclusively in a material way? In the greatest feats of clairvoyance, there are always those who refuse to believe what they see or hear, who insist that only coincidence or fraud can explain what has been shown to them. In the most spectacular instances of spiritual healing, the same responses hold, the verdict is that he would have got better anyway. If he isn't improved, then that is used to discredit all spiritual healing."

There was a note of frustration in Olga's voice that was strangely moving. Quite unexpectedly I found myself saying, "Olga, I don't mean to heckle you. It's just that I'm trying so hard to stick to logic and cold facts."

"Don't you worry, honey," she promptly replied. "I've been living with this kind of heckling all my life. People have eyes but don't see; they have ears but won't listen. When I made my commitment to do spiritual healing, I was fully aware of the skepticism and ridicule and even occasional hostility which it would entail. But healing is God's gift to me—and I will not bury the talent he has given into my keeping. And not only will I go on healing, but I will also go on working with scientists in the hope and faith that by dint of sheer weight of the accumulated evidence, someday, somehow, the limitations of this physical world will be manifest to all and a glimpse of the other world will shine through."

It was quite a speech that Olga made and it provided me with a surprising revelation. The selflessness and wholeheartedness of her healing ministry had been apparent almost from the start. Now, however, I was also aware of the tremendous courage involved in its pursuit, too. Such a unique and praiseworthy combination, it seemed to me, as much as any of the experiments in which she had participated, should in the final analysis be deemed the most conclusive and convincing test of all.

CHAPTER X

The Prosecution Rests

THE scientific approach to everything, which permeates so much of modern life, tends to obliterate the fact that research can be, and often is an end in itself. There is an underlying, fallacious feeling that any thorough investigation is unsuccessful unless it produces conclusions which follow from it as inevitably as the day follows the night. There is the further, utterly unrealistic expectation that these conclusions must therefore be nailed to the door of the world by the researchers with the declaration: "Here I stand. I can do no other."

It was with these misconceptions, in any case, that I had originally embarked upon my Worrall research. Because of them, I had been ridiculously sure that, given sufficient facts and time, a perfect answer to the psychic riddle would come forth the way the sum total of a whole series of complex numbers emerges from an adding machine when you push the right button. Because of them, I almost lost sight of the basic purpose of my self-appointed task: to "go back and tell" what I was "hearing and seeing"; to testify, but not necessarily to conclude.

As usual, it was Olga who understood this aspect of the whole project long before I. As word of my Worrall research and book spread, the principal question which I encountered almost unfailingly was, "Well, Edwina, now that you've gone on this occult kick and are checking it all out, do you really go along with all that stuff? How about it?" And when, in reply, I honestly confessed that I still didn't know what to think—that I was tremendously impressed but by no means totally convinced—the visible reaction of disappointment and disbelief was as conspicuous as a flag flying at half-mast.

Only Olga remained unperturbed at my inability or unwillingness to make any definite commitments. "Honey," she told me repeatedly, when I talked about this to her, "your personal opinions don't really matter. Sure, they want your verdict about it all—if you had any to give—but that doesn't mean they would accept it. They're just hungry for something to believe. My mission is to do and your job is to tell it as it is. That's enough."

The question nevertheless persisted in my mind: was it enough? I yearned to tie up the whole project with a big, bold stamp of approval—or disapproval—like a side of beef. To flounder, instead, in a sea of uncertainty left me with an unhappy and uncomfortable feeling of having labored long, but in vain.

"I know what!" Olga said suddenly one day, sensing my mood during a visit when I was there to check some facts I had incorporated into one of my chapters. "As I told you before, your conversion is absolutely unimportant. But, since you're still apparently looking for answers, why don't you read some more material that Ambrose and I prepared just a little while back? It's just occurred to me—while we were speaking—that everything I've been telling you about spiritual healing and clairvoyance and the entire psychic world has been *me* speaking, *my* experience, *my* presentation. How would you like some biblical corroboration?"

"What do you mean?" I responded.

"Just what I said," Olga replied. "The Bible contains the most amazing history of psychic phenomena that has ever been produced." She stood up as she spoke and went to her files. "You know," she laughed, "these files are so full—Ambrose used to say I was a hoarder, but I must have known that you'd come looking into them someday." Then she turned back to me with a thickish bundle of papers, held together by two rubber bands, and said earnestly: "Here, Edwina child. Take these. It's an outline of almost all the psychic manifestations recorded in the Bible. Read this and get some more food for thought."

"More food for thought?" I repeated, as I took the papers. "Are you sure I won't wind up with mental indigestion?"

Olga smiled in acknowledgment of my half-joking remark. Then she answered thoughtfully, "You know, people act as if psychic happenings are some recent perversions of oldtime witchcraft. Few individuals seem to realize that spirit voices, automatic writing, clairvoyance, and all the rest of the occult gambit appear again and again in both the Old and the New Testaments. I always feel like saying to those who stand ready to cast the first stone, 'Have you read the Bible?'"

"Well, I have read the Bible, Olga," I replied immediately, "and I never thought of it as at all supportive of psychic phenomena. In fact, if I remember correctly, isn't there something in the Old Testament that warns against soothsayers, diviners—"

"—and necromancers," Olga finished for me. "You're absolutely right. It's in Deuteronomy. But to take that as an absolute prohibition is to take it entirely out of context. The Israelites were told to beware of such—that's true—but not because the principle was wrong, but because there were *false* prophets among them. In fact, they were also informed at the same time that God would raise up, from among them, a *true* Prophet to whom they were instructed to listen."

"And what about the New Testament?" I asked next, unable to remember any specifics myself.

"The New Testament almost lays out the whole course," Olga declared emphatically. "Not only is there nothing against spiritual gifts, but Paul in his first letter to the Corinthians describes the different ways in which they may be manifested in people. Edwina, she interrupted herself, reaching out and retrieving the papers in my hand, "let me read you that part right now. Ambrose and I included it right at the beginning, if I remember correctly, and"—she was undoing the rubber bands and searching for the page while she spoke—"here it is. Now listen, and listen carefully."

"Psychic powers," Olga read aloud, "are certain kinds of mental abilities which, when exercised, produce unusual results often referred to as 'psychic phenomena.'

"Psychic phenomena may result from the exercise of the mental abilities of a person living in a physical body, sometimes referred to as an embodied person; or from the mental abilities of a person not so embodied. Even groups of such persons, both embodied and discarnate, may jointly be responsible for psychic phemonena.

"These mental abilities are spiritual gifts. You will find them described by Paul in his first letter to the Corinthians, chapter twelve, verses one through eleven.

"Now concerning spiritual gifts, brethren, I would not have you ignorant. Ye know that ye were Gentiles, carried away unto these dumb idols, even as ye were led. Wherefore I give you to understand, that no man speaking by the Spirit of God calleth Jesus accursed: and that no man can say that Jesus is the Lord but by the Holy Ghost. Now there are diversities of gifts but the same Spirit. And there are differences of administrations, but the same Lord. And there are diversities of operations, but it is the same God which worketh all in all. But the manifestation of the Spirit is given to every man to profit withal. For to one is given by the Spirit the word of wisdom; to another the word of knowledge by the same Spirit; To another faith by the same Spirit; to another the gifts of healing by the same Spirit; To another the working of miracles; to another prophecy; to another discerning of spirits; to another divers kinds of tongues; to another the interpretation of tongues; But all these worketh that one and the selfsame Spirit, dividing to every man severally as he will."

When she came to the end of this passage, Olga paused for a moment and then said, "This description by Paul is very brief, but if you go through all of the Holy Bible, there is much detailed information on psychic events that covers a period of about fifteen hundred years. That's what Ambrose and I tried to outline in these pages." She gave the papers back to me and sighed. "The list is in here and the passages; but you can check it out in the Bible for yourself."

"I will," I promised—and I did.

Almost as soon as I arrived home, I began delving into the papers I had brought from Olga's. It was indeed an amazing and fascinating list and I verified each citation with the biblical source just as I had said I would: there were no errors. In brief, the outline reads as follows:

Some References to Psychic Phenomena Recorded in the Holy Bible

Phenomena	Book	Chapter	Verse
Clairvoyance:	1 Samuel	2	27
	1 Samuel	9	15, 16, 17, 18, 19, 20
	Daniel	10	7, 8, 9
	John	1	48
	John	4	16, 18
	Acts	8	26
Spirit control:	1 Samuel	10	6
	Ezekiel	2	2
	Ezekiel	3	24
	Ezekiel	8	1, 3
	2 Peter	1	21
	1 John	4	1

Phenomena	Book	Chapter	Verse
Spirit voices:	Genesis	22	11, 12
	Exodus	3	4
	Judges	6	20
	Judges	13	3
	1 Samuel	3	10
	1 Kings	19	7, 13
	Daniel	4	31
	Luke	1	28
	Luke	2	9, 10, 11, 12, 13, 14
	Luke	9	35
	John 12	12	28
	Acts	9	4, 5, 7
	Acts	10	13, 15
	Revelation	1	10
Messages from departed spirits:	1 Samuel	28	19
	Luke	9	30, 31
	Acts	22	17, 18
	Revelation	1	17, 18
	Revelation	22	9
Spirit return:	Matthew	17	3
Levitation and transportation of the physical body:	2 Kings	11	11
	Ezekiel	8	3
	Matthew	14	29
	Acts	1	9
	Acts	8	39
Trance:	Numbers	24	4
	Ezekiel	4	24
	Daniel	8	18
	Daniel	10	9
	Acts	10	10
	Acts	22	17

Phenomena	Book	Chapter	Verse
Psychic protection against fire:	Isaiah	6	6, 7
	Daniel	3	25, 27
	Mark	16	18
Sounds from spiritual realm:	Ezekiel	3	13
	John	12	29
	Acts	2	2
	Revelation	11	19
Celestial music and musical instruments:	Revelation	1	10
	Revelation	14	2
	Revelation	14	2
	Revelation	15	2, 3
Locating lost objects:	1 Samuel	9	20
	Matthew	17	27
	John	21	6
Touched by spirit or discarnate hand:	Daniel	8	18
	Daniel	10	10
	Revelation	1	17, 18
Independent writing:	Daniel	5	5
	Exodus	24	12
	Exodus	31	18
	Exodus	32	16
	Exodus	34	1
	Deuteronomy	5	22
	Deuteronomy	9	10
Automatic writing:	1 Chronicles	28	19
Materialization:	Genesis	3	8
	Genesis	18	1, 2
	Genesis	32	24
	Exodus	24	10
	Joshua	5	13, 14

Phenomena	Book	Chapter	Verse
	Judges	6	11, 21
	1 Samuel	28	13, 14
	Ezekiel	8	3
	Daniel	3	25
	Daniel	5	5
	Daniel	6	10
	Daniel	9	21
	Mark	16	5, 6, 9, 12, 14
	Luke	24	15, 30, 31, 36
	John	20	12, 14, 19
	John	21	1
	Acts	10	3, 19
	Revelation	13	17, 18
Spirit manifestations, in luminous clouds and flames of fire:	Genesis	15	17
	Exodus	3	2
	Exodus	13	21
	Exodus	34	30
	Exodus	40	34
	Leviticus	9	24
	Numbers	16	35
	Judges	6	21
	Judges	13	30
	1 Kings	18	38
	1 Kings	19	11, 12
	2 Kings	1	10, 12
	1 Chronicles	21	26
	2 Chronicles	7	1, 2
	Matthew	17	2
	Mark	9	3, 7
	Luke	9	30, 31, 35
	Acts	2	3
	Acts	12	7
	Acts	26	13

Phenomena	Book	Chapter	Verse
Speaking through trumpet:	Exodus	19	13, 16, 19
	Exodus	20	18
	Revelation	1	10
Spirit communications in dreams:	Job	33	15
	Joel	2	28
	Genesis	28	12
	Genesis	31	24
	Genesis	37	5
	Genesis	41	17

When, after several days, I completed my research on this list, I turned next to the biblical examples of spiritual healing. The text, in this connection, begins:

"We will discuss one more spiritual gift, the gift of healing. There are many schools of thought on this subject. There are those who believe that sickness is punishment for something that occurred in some previous life and that it is wrong to alleviate suffering because it interferes with the person's 'karma.' If this were a true philosophy, we should have no healing physicians, medicines, pain relievers, or hospitals. First aid would never be administered, and there would be no need for worldwide health organizations.

"There are records of spiritual healings dating back over a period of five thousand years. Moses, Elisha, Elijah, Jesus, and many others demonstrated the gift of healing. Healings have taken place in shrines and temples without the benefit of any intermediary psychic or medium. This indicates that it is right to heal. Healing is an inborn capability of the body. It can be accelerated by proper treatment, by physicians and spiritual healing."

After this introduction, several extensive lists of Old and

New Testament healings are set forth—and of these, surprisingly, only the healings by Jesus and his disciples were familiar to me. Most of the Old Testament references were comparatively unknown—at least, as such. They are in part:

Abimelech's household healed:	Genesis chapter 20
Miriam healed of leprosy:	Numbers 12: 1, 16
Moses heals serpent's bites:	Numbers 21: 4, 9
Jeroboam healed:	1 Kings 13:6
Elijah heals the widow's son:	1 Kings 17: 19-20
Elisha heals the son of the Shunammite:	2 Kings 4: 32-34
Naaman the Syrian is healed of leprosy by Elisha:	2 Kings 5: 9, 10, 14
King Hezekiah healed by Isaiah:	2 Kings 20: 1-11
	Isaiah 38: 1-6
The healing of Job:	Job 42: 1-17
Nebuchadnezzar healed of mental illness:	Daniel 4: 34-37

About the time I finished checking all the material that had been handed to me and while I was still chewing it over, Olga called to invite me to a party that was being given in her honor.

"I don't recall if I told you," she said, sounding quite pleased, "but I've been out to California last week, getting me an honorary degree—Doctor of Humane Letters—from the Church of Religious Science Institute. That's their seminary, you know. Anyway, some friends are having a dinner here in Baltimore to celebrate. Can you come? It's this Friday night—at the Broadview."

"I'd love to," I answered promptly. "I need a breather from book-writing and, frankly, I'm still reeling from that final mass of biblical stuff which you and Ambrose have compiled. It certainly makes you stop and think."

"Quit thinking," Olga advised cheerfully. "Remember what I told you? Just tell it as it is; your opinion isn't even relevant. What makes you think what you are writing about would have greater weight if it bore your seal of approval? Honey, they mostly didn't believe Jesus when he told them about the things of this world. They don't much really believe psychics when we tell them about the things of heaven. So why expect them to believe you?"

Why indeed? I was still wondering about this when I went to the party, which turned out to be a very pleasant and happy affair: good food, lots of laughter, and about twenty congenial participants.

"Speech! Speech!" they teased Olga after the dessert had been served, and laughingly, she responded with, "Unaccustomed as I am to public speaking—" Then she stopped suddenly and said, "All I can say is thankyou. Ambrose and I both thank you. Whatever honors me, honors him, too."

With these words, a more serious feeling evolved throughout the whole group. "It's five minutes before nine o'clock," someone reminded the others out loud, and in a matter of seconds, a semicircle of chairs, with one for Olga in the middle of the open half, was set up in the adjoining room.

"Good," said Olga, as she seated herself. "Sit down and let's have my silent time. All lights off, please, except one lamp in that far corner." Then, closing her eyes in the dimness, she prayed: "Gracious Father, we again approach the pure light of thy spirit and we are cleansed by its powerful rays. The channels of our being are opened and through them flow the living waters from thy Spirit. The thirsty ones that turn to thee at this time will be able to drink deeply of the life-giving fluids and they shall be restored to perfect health in accordance with thy laws. For this we give our thanks in his name. We are grateful for the privilege of being reflectors of thy Light, for we know that along those reflected beams, thy healing power flows— and those who are touched will receive and be blessed. And for those of thy children who are made whole at this time, we give our thanks."

In the silence which followed these few sentences, we all sat with closed eyes. There was no movement, no sound—only a kind of all-pervasive, meaningful quiet that filled the comparatively small room with the peace and solemnity of a great cathedral.

After several minutes of this concentrated prayer, Olga spoke again. "Thank you, Father, for your presence here with us tonight, and for thy healing power which has been so graciously bestowed and so gratefully received." Then, after a brief pause and in an entirely different, more conversational tone of voice, she said: "David, I see your mother standing beside your chair. She is very happy. She says that it is her birthday today, and she is so pleased because you not only remembered it but put on her ring, which she had left to you, in honor of the occasion. She says you hesitated about doing it, but then did."

As Olga finished this "message," a middle-aged gray-haired man, about five chairs to my left, exclaimed happily: "It is Mother's birthday today and I did put on her ring,"—and he held up his hand to show the ring—"because I thought she would like me to. I wasn't sure it wasn't a silly gesture, though, so I didn't even mention it to my wife. Oh, thank you, Mother, for your message—and thank you, Olga, for giving it to me!"

The moment David finished speaking, Olga began another communication, This time for the woman sitting beside me who, judging from what was said, had been recently widowed. "Dick is right behind you," Olga stated matter-of-factly, and his hands are resting on your shoulders. He says to tell you he is very proud of you—of how you're getting on by yourself and with the children."

Olga was silent for a moment and I was certain she did not hear the woman whisper to me or to herself: "That was his way, his special way to show approval—to stand behind my chair and put his hands lovingly upon my shoulders."

Then Olga continued with a note of puzzlement in her voice. "That's funny," she said. "He's laughing now and taking his mustache on and off—as if it were fake. He insists you'll understand."

"Oh, I do! I do!" The woman was almost beside herself with excitement. "It was always our private joke. I hated his mustache and used to try to get him to shave it off because it tickled when he kissed me. And when he did take it off, he grew it right back. Oh my darling, I understand! I do!"

"Well," Olga concluded, "he wants you to know that he still has his mustache. And he keeps laughing about it as he talks."

For nearly a full half-hour after this, Olga delivered messages around the room. Mary's grandmother wanted her family to know that she no longer had a limp; Bob's father was back with Mother once more and happy; Jean's Uncle Archibald wanted to remind his niece again that he had been a physician and to encourage her to go on with her plans to enter medical school the coming fall—he would impress her parents to cooperate all the way.

On and on Olga went in this fashion. Some people made immediate comment but most merely acknowledged the communications so that I could not gauge the evidentiary significance of each statement. What I could determine, however, was the overall reaction in the room. We were still in the half-light, obviously, but there was an almost visible glow that had come into the place and illuminated everyone there the way the sun does when it breaks through some dark clouds. Happiness has its own shine, I know, and happiness was present on almost every face—but it was more than that: it was hope and fulfillment, as well, and a kind of suppressed excitement.

When the session was over and I was ready to leave, I made a point to tell Olga what I had seen; how pleased and surprised I was at what had occurred. Her response, essentially, was one of surprise at my surprise.

"I keep forgetting," she exclaimed, "that you're just a new-comer to any of this. Not that I always plunge into clairvoy-ance at the drop of a hat! But when it comes spontaneously, as it did tonight, then I feel privileged to transmit messages from those in the spirit world to their loved ones here. It always means so much to both sides—and we had so many spirit visitors with us this evening!"

"I could see how much it means," I agreed; "at least to the people here. I don't think I will ever forget the looks on their faces as they heard in this way from someone who was gone. They were so obviously moved, so delighted, so—"

"My goodness!" Olga interrupted me as I groped for adjec-tives. "If you think these people in this little bit were such a sight to behold, you should see what happens at one of our big healing services during a conference. In fact, now that I think of it, why don't you?"

"Why don't I what?" I asked, not sure of where Olga was heading next.

"Why don't you come with me to the conference meeting tomorrow?" Olga explained. "I'm driving up to nearby Penn-sylvania to take part in a large healing service which will be held in a Protestant church. I know you've been to the New Life Clinic many times, but this will be a different kind of thing. It will be the end of a five-day conference on spiritual healing. It's a climactic occasion with several priests and minis-ters taking part in the healing and there should be at least five or six hundred people present. Okay?"

There were in fact closer to one thousand people gathered in the church for the service which I went to with Olga the next evening. I sat down in a middle pew while Olga went off to join the clergymen who were waiting in the anteroom for the service to begin. There was, in the twenty-minute interval, ample opportunity for me to look all around.

The church itself was a fairly modern building. Every seat in the place was filled—including chairs that had been added to every row and throughout the entire back and the entry foyer. The people seated throughout represented every segment of life: men, women, children; young, older, aged, and even a few infants in arms.

There was no levity visible, none of the usual Sunday-go-to-meetin' kind of sociability. Many sat with their eyes closed, their lips silently praying. It was as if each person were self-contained in a separate cell at the same time that all present were joined together in a communion that had undeniable, indescribable elements of holiness.

At seven o'clock sharp, Olga, wearing her long black robe, came solemnly down the aisle, followed by two priests and three ministers. After one brief hymn, Olga came forward to address the congregation.

"We are not the usual church gathering here tonight," she began. "We have come to obey the Master's command to 'go heal the sick.' We have come to do as he did, trusting in his promise that those who believe will do even greater things yet.

"Behind us is the long history of spiritual healing which men of God have done in the Old and the New Testaments. Remember how Elisha the prophet restored a sick child to health: how he 'lay upon the child and put his mouth upon the child's mouth and his eyes upon his eyes and his hands upon his hands and stretched himself upon him'? Remember how Jesus healed all who came to him for help: the paralytic carried by four men; the sick man at the pool of Bethesda; the woman with the issue of blood? Remember how he raised Lazarus from the dead and the daughter of Jairus—and how the record tells that 'all who touched him were healed'? Remember the many healings by the disciples, armed only by their faith and the word of Jesus when he sent out, first the Twelve, and then the Seventy? Remember the raising of Tabitha, the miracles of Stephen, the healings at Samaria by Philip?

"I remember—these and many more. But I also remember the disbelief and ridicule which have surrounded spiritual gifts and spiritual healing since the early church. Men have forgotten that God is spirit and that man is created in the image of God. Man's mind is a reflection of the Universal Mind, which is God. The Universal Laws of God cannot be broken; they always operate; they do not fail; they never change.

"Jesus demonstrated this but comparatively few would listen. He emphasized life beyond the grave. He pleaded with his people to believe: 'Verily, verily, I say unto you, he that heareth my word and believeth on Him that sent me, hath everlasting life.' He went so far as to demonstrate this fact in his resurrection, knowing only too well—as he had told the nobleman of Capernaum: 'Except ye see signs and wonders, ye will not believe.'

"Well, I can tell you that today we can see signs and wonders and so-called miracles for ourselves—for the laws that govern their demonstration are universal, everlasting, and unchangeable. When I feel a breast tumor, scheduled for surgery, reduce to half its size under my touch; or when I see a man suddenly regain his hearing with a 'pop' after a laying-on of hands; or when I learn that following a spiritual treatment, a terminal cancer patient had no more pain and went on gradually to a complete recovery—then I know that these are the self-same signs and wonders of which Jesus spoke. And I also know that these things are old, not new; natural, not supernatural; normal, not abnormal; fulfillment, not circumvention of God's universal, immutable laws which were, are and always will be available to all."

At this point in her brief sermon, Olga paused. Then she concluded: "There will eternally be skeptics who 'seeing, see not; and hearing they hear not, neither do they understand.' But the spirit of Truth has come as Jesus promised it would.

We know this and that is why we are here. 'Blessed are your
eyes, for they see; and your ears for they hear . . . many
prophets and righteous men have desired to see those things
which ye see and have not seen them; and to hear those things
which ye hear and have not heard them.' Come now, whoever
has a need. Every healing service is an experiment. It is God
who heals. Come and let us all see what happens!"

And how they came! They moved in two orderly lines down
the middle aisle of the church—and the procession seemed
endless. Patiently, expectantly they moved slowly forward,
waiting their turns to go up and stand before Olga and the
clergymen who stood at the altar rail for the laying-on of
hands.

As they waited, silently and prayerfully, the organ played
softly in the background, one hymn after another. At first, the
music and the rustling of the moving lines of people were all
that were heard: on and on they came, literally by the hundreds, seemingly as continuous as the waves of the ocean.
After a long while, though, as the organist broke into the
strains of the old, familiar song, "How Great Thou Art," a
beautiful thing happened. Obviously without any premedita-
tion or plan, those people who were already returned to their
seats after having been to the altar rail, began to hum the
melody of the hymn softly—not to sing the words, but merely
to carry the tune almost under their breath. Before long, the
soft humming spread throughout the entire church. Over and
over again the hymn was sung, and like the murmuring of a
gentle wind, it filled the sanctuary with a sweet, inspiring
sound.

More than anything else, though, I could not turn my eyes
away from the expressions on the faces of those all about me.
I watched, fascinated, acutely aware of what Olga had meant
when she had assured me that I had seen nothing of what
spiritual power could do for people until I had seen a group

such as this. What hope was mirrored in their eyes, what joy was revealed in the curve of their lips! It was all that I had seen at Olga's party the night before, but now of such magnitude that it was like a vibrant, tangible, pulsating force which swept everything and everyone before it.

I was not only moved. I was enlightened. Suddenly I could understand what Olga had been repeatedly telling me: all that mattered was that the word be spread. For me, as yet, there had been no moment of final truth and might never be. Perhaps this in itself was but symptomatic of what ails us generally as a civilization and a people—that few of us are ever so blessed. Rarely does a cross flame in the sky to compel our conversion and even more rarely does the voice of God call out aloud. Mostly, we wrestle inside ourselves with our indecision and engage in an endless search for what we can believe that lasts a lifetime.

Olga Worrall, however, had found answers. She had not merely found them but she *was* prepared to nail them on the doors of the world for all to see. She was generous enough to share them with all who would listen; she was courageous enough to defend them against all challenge—and I had seen for myself what these answers could do for people.

Sitting there in that crowded church, surrounded by the exhilaration and happiness and hope that those answers had wrought, I realized that Olga was right. It was definitely enough for me to "tell it as it is" and to tell it all. When it was told—and that was exactly what I determined then and there to do!—then, as Olga herself would surely say when she heard: "Who hath ears to hear, let him hear."